IT LOOKS BETTER IN 3D

The Reality-First Approach to Childhood
Screen Use

Dr. Catherine L'Ecuyer

To Alicia, Gabriel, Nicolas, and Juliette.

A father is out hiking in the mountains with his two teenagers. Once they reach the top, they wonder at the view:
'Look, kids, what a gorgeous sunset!'
'Honestly, Dad? Two hours of walking to `
see a screensaver?!'
Adapted from a *Faro* cartoon

Table of Contents

A Word from the Author:
How Much Screen Time Is Too Much?

Everyone is entitled to his own opinion, but not to his own facts.
Daniel P. Moynihan, American sociologist

Over the course of the second half of the last century, television made significant inroads into the households of most developed countries. In 1970, American children had their first contact with screens at the age of 4.[1] Their access to technology was then limited to television and radio, which had a relatively slow pace and rhythm. Now, 50 years later, American children have access to a wide range of electronic devices with fast-paced content from the time they are 4 months old.[2]

A 2016 report from Statistics Canada revealed that Canadian children between the ages of 3 and 4 spent an average of 2 hours per day in front of a screen,[3] and nearly a quarter of five-year-old children were exposed to more than 2 hours of screen use per day.[4] More specifically, in Quebec, a 2019 study on sixth-grade Montreal students indicated that a fifth of them used screens for 4 hours of their free time each day (which excludes the use of technology in class or for homework).[5]

---

[1] American Academy of Pediatrics. (2016). Children and adolescents and digital media. *Pediatrics, 138*(5), e20162593.

[2] *Ibid.*

[3] Statistics Canada. (2016). Table 2 Sample characteristics, household population aged 3 to 4, Canada, excluding territories, 2009 to 2013 (combined).

[4] Statistics Canada. (2016b). Table 4 Adherence to physical activity and screen-time guidelines, by age group and selected characteristics, household population aged 3 to 5, Canada, 2009 to 2013 (combined).

[5] Biron, J., Fournier, M., Tremblay, P., & Nguyen, C.T. (2019). *Les écrans et la santé de la population à Montréal.* Montréal: Direction régionale de santé publique du CIUSS du Centre-Sud-de-l'Île-de-Montréal, p. 10.

In the United Kingdom, a 2018 study[6] reported that three quarters of children under 5 have access to a computer or tablet and almost half of them own one.

In the United States, a 2017 report by Common Sense Media[7] found that on average, children under the age of 2 used digital media for an hour and a half per day. A report published by the same organization in 2019[8] found that children between the ages of 8 and 12 spend 4 hours and 44 minutes per day and teenagers between 13 and 18 years of age spend 7 hours and 22 minutes per day using digital technology, not including time spent on screens at school or while doing homework. According to the same study, 53% of youth have a smartphone by the age of 11 and 69% by the age of 12.

And there you have it. ***In 2019, the average North American teenager spent over 7 hours per day in front of a screen.*** That is 2689 hours per year spent in front of a screen. If we exclude time spent sleeping, that adds up to about half the year. Although incredible, these numbers speak for themselves: ***young people spend almost half of their waking hours in front of a screen.*** And if we add up the amount of screen time to which youth between 8 and 18 years old are exposed, we will realize that ***they spend a cumulative total of 4 years and 3 months of the waking hours of their adolescence online.***

If we do the math, the average high school graduate will have had about 24,771 hours of screen time over the course of his or her school years, which is about 2.6 times the number of

[6] Childwise. (2018). *Childwise Monitor pre-school report.*

[7] Common Sense Media. (2017). Fact sheet. The Common Sense census: Media use by kids age zero to eight. https://www.commonsensemedia.org/research/the-common-sense-census-media-use-by-kids-age-zero-to-eight-2017

[8] Rideout, V., & Robb, M.B. (2019). The Common Sense census: Media use by tweens and teens. San Francisco, CA: Common Sense Media.

hours (9432[9]) spent in class during the same period! And this figure excludes time spent using technology at school or at home while doing homework and does not account for the number of hours that children will have spent on screens as a result of the coronavirus pandemic.

These are surprising statistics, because when we add to them the time that children and teenagers devote to studying, sleeping, eating, daily hygiene, etc., we end up with a daily average that far surpasses the 24 hours in a day.[10] Why? Time is not flexible. How can this be possible?

The answer is that children are using their screens while multitasking, which means that they are using several devices at once, or that they are using technology while doing something else. According to the 2019 study by Common Sense Media that we cited above,[11] almost half of youth between the ages of 13 and 18 listen to music while doing their homework, almost a quarter text while doing so, and almost a fifth use social media or have the television on while they work. So, while they are doing their homework, they read and respond to a message on Instagram; while playing video games, they chat with their friends online; while eating, they watch television and talk with their parents. Do these children of the digital age have the ability to process multiple sources of information at once? We might be tempted to respond, "Of course, they were born in the digital

---

[9] The annual average number of mandatory teaching hours in OECD countries is 802 hours per year in primary schools and 924 hours in secondary, according to the report *Panorama de la educación, Indicadores de la OCDE* (2013), from the Ministry of Education, Culture and Sport of the Government of Spain. Retrieved from http://www.oecd.org/education/Panorama%20de%20la%20educacion%202013.pdf

[10] Childwise. (2014). Childwise pocket fact sheet, Key facts about children and young people in the UK.

[11] Rideout, V., & Robb, M.B. (2019). The Common Sense census: Media use by tweens and teens. San Francisco, CA: Common Sense Media.

age." This seems to imply that they have some sort of superpower that allows them to engage in several activities at once; something we as "digital immigrants" can only aspire to. But is this really the case?

In the following pages, this book aims to dismantle several of the myths about screen use that circulate with impunity, and that only serve to increase the amount of time that our children and students spend using technology. This book addresses several pro-technology arguments that it is often taboo to refute, or even address. We have undoubtedly heard certain arguments in favour of technology use during childhood and adolescence, both at home and at school, such as:

> "It's the future!"

> "We can't let them miss the boat when it comes to technology."

> "We should adapt to the learning methods of the digital generation."

> "Technology in classrooms is a must, it engages students, and therefore contributes to their learning."

> "Children born in the digital age are capable of media multitasking."

> "Technology helps children to focus and motivates them to learn."

> "It's the future, whether you like it or not."

> "Oh, those technophobes and alarmists who want to limit access to technology!"

We will discuss the most common misconceptions about technology use in education ("technomyths"), notably in regard to media multitasking, "digital natives," the neutrality of technology, and the digital divide. We will also discuss the confusion between *sustained attention* and *fascination*, the economic interests at play, some consequences of sustained screen use for children and teenagers, as well as recommendations from the principal pediatric associations.

During the exceptional circumstances brought about by the COVID-19 pandemic, increased screen use may be justifiable. Especially during times of lockdown, screens have made it possible for children to communicate with their friends and family and connect with their schools, among other uses. However, the pandemic has also contributed to the acquisition of bad habits and aggravated some of the existing abuses in regard to technology use. Now, more than ever, it is necessary to take stock of the circumstances surrounding this use.

This book is not intended to be "alarmist," "technophobic," or to point the finger. Technology is a marvelous tool when the user is prepared to use it wisely. Our children will obviously end up using it when they have a real need for it and are ready to use it. But how will they prepare themselves for this? Contrary to popular opinion, and as will be demonstrated throughout this book, the best preparation for the virtual world does not involve the use of electronic devices, but rather the personal experience gained from contact with the real world.

In continuation of *The Wonder Approach*, the book that you have in your hands is intended as a reprieve from the demanding task of educating; a relieving interlude; a moment of reflection allowing parents, often overwhelmed by the technology question, to understand what is happening, to better grasp the implications and consequences of this new phenomenon in our classrooms and homes. Far from giving "ready-made formulas," it is meant to equip parents and teachers with tools for making free and informed decisions about education, in light of the most recent studies.

Dear reader, I wish you an enjoyable read!

Chapter 1
Multitasking and the "Digital Native"

There is time enough for everything, in the course of the day, if you do but one thing at once; but there is not time enough in the year, if you will do two things at a time.
Advice given by Philip Stanhope, Earl of Chesterfield, to his son

The term "digital native," coined by Mark Prensky, describes one who, because he or she was born in the digital age (after 1984), is accustomed to receiving and processing information better than those born before that era (the so-called "digital immigrants"). According to this "hypothesis," digital natives have cognitive advantages that positively affect their learning relative to the generation that precedes them, notably in regard to media multitasking.

Multitasking is one of the great promises of our time, especially in the digital era. It is only logical. If you can do two things at once, you can do them in half the time, or else you can do multiple things in the time that it would otherwise take to do just one. This is naturally very interesting to us, because this new way of working and directing our attention seems to come with the promise of better time management, and thus an increase in productivity.

However, an analyst at the business-research firm Basex estimated that multitasking cost the American economy 650 billion dollars in 2007 alone, due to the resulting loss in productivity.[12] How is this possible?

---

[12] Sohr, S. (2007, March 25). Slow down, brave multitasker, and don't read this in traffic. *The New York Times.* https://www.nytimes.com/2007/03/25/business/25multi.html

Can we engage in two activities at once? Can someone chew bubble gum while walking? If this person has learned to walk and has had practice doing it, and if it is not the first time that he or she is chewing gum, the response is affirmative, because the two activities are relatively automatic. They do not require information processing but are performed naturally, like sneezing or yawning. That said, is it possible to simultaneously carry out two or more activities that require our attention? For example, can we read our emails, listen to the news on the radio, and watch a movie, while at the same time answering the phone and taking care of a child? We can doubtlessly be *physically* present for each of these activities, but can we really carry them all out at the same time while being *mentally* present for each of them?

What psychologists and neuroscientists have systematically repeated over the course of the last 20 years, and what no evidence has refuted, is that **activities that require information processing cannot be performed simultaneously or in parallel**. They must rather be carried out sequentially.

In order to go from one activity to another, we must turn our attention away from one task in order to refocus it on the other. And if we perform several tasks at once, we oscillate between them, but we not carry them out in parallel. In short, multitasking, far from holding promise, is a myth, a popular belief that has firmly taken root in our society. This myth is fed by the belief that digital natives outperform adults in multitasking, which is false. They too oscillate between their various technological activities and this oscillation costs them as much as it does adults.

Despite its popularity, this concept has been called into question by several studies since 2008. Specifically, *The Google Generation: The Information Behaviour of the Researcher of the Future*, a report published in 2011 by various scholars, found that the characteristics attributed to digital natives have been overestimated. While it may be true that "young people demonstrate an apparent ease and familiarity with computers, they rely heavily on search engines, view rather than read and do not possess the critical and analytical skills to assess the information that they find on the web."[13] In conclusion, the report overturns the theory that the "Google generation" is the most web-literate.

In 2017, a literature review on the concept, "digital native,"[14] concluded that it had no scientific support. **The belief that a person born in the digital age has a greater ability to focus attention on many sources of information simultaneously is a myth.**

However, despite these data, we continue to think that digital natives do better than their parents in this regard. We fall back on the argument of neural plasticity (the brain's ability to change and adapt as a result of experience) and the neuromyth of infinite intelligence (which we will allude to in the next chapter), thinking that our children can "adapt to anything."

Although it is true that the human being has a great capacity for adapting to its environment, an overly simplistic application of the brain plasticity concept in the educational context can lead to misinterpretation. There is in fact no evidence supporting the claims that technology is rewiring our brains.[15]

---

13 Rowlands, I., Nicholas, D., Williams, P., Huntington, P., Fieldhouse, M., Gunter, B., & Tenopir, C. (2008). The Google generation: The information behaviour of the researcher of the future. *Aslib Proceedings, Vol. 60*. Emerald Group Publishing Limited.

14 Kirschner, P.A., & De Bruyckere, P. (2017). The myths of the digital native and the multitasker. *Teaching and Teacher Education, 67*, 135–142.

15 Wilmer, H.H., Sherman, L.E., & Chein, J.M. (2017). Smartphones and cognition: A review of research exploring the links between mobile technology habits and cognitive functioning. *Frontiers in Psychology, 8*, p. 605.

However, intelligence and memory have their limits, and as a report by the Organization of American States indicates, so does plasticity. Beyond these limits, stimuli can induce changes that compromise learning:

> Nonetheless, the shift of concepts from plasticity to the educational context allows for and even fosters [mis]interpretations of it. Plasticity has its limits. The tensions to which the individual is subjected force him to adapt, and this is attainable within margins, beyond which the stimulus inducing change becomes dangerous and may compromise his integrity.[16]

But perhaps we still think: "OK, sure, they can't do multiple things at once. But because they do it so much and so often, it makes sense that they would do better than us when multitasking." We might also think that they must have a better working memory (the memory that retains one or several tasks while we turn our attention to another), that they must oscillate more quickly from one task to another (shifting their focus away from and back to each task), and that they must be better at filtering out irrelevant information. At least, that is the popular belief, is it not? But is it true?

In 2007, a study carried out at Stanford University[17] tested these three hypotheses. It analyzed whether certain university students, who regularly engaged in heavy media multitasking, performed better than those who did not, in the following parameters:

1. Working memory;

---

[16] Executive Secretariat for Integral Development: Department of Education and Culture. (2007). Understanding the state of the art in early childhood education and care: The first three years of life.

[17] Ophir, E., Nass, C., & Wagner, A.D. (2009). Cognitive control in media multitaskers. *Proceedings of the National Academy of Sciences of the United States of America, 106*(37), 15.583–15.587.

2. The ability to adeptly oscillate attention between various tasks;

3. The capacity to filter information by determining what is relevant and what is not (*criteria of relevancy*).

So, in which of these areas did those who engaged in intensive media multitasking perform better? The data collected demonstrated that *the heavy multitaskers had worse results in each of the three parameters.* **The consequence of multitasking while working is that we pay less attention to any one of the various activities we try to do at the same time**, because we must recover the sequence of ideas required by each thought every time that we shift our attention from one activity to another. This is why Herbert Simon, winner of the Nobel Prize in Economics, said, "What information consumes is rather obvious: it consumes the attention of its recipients. Hence a wealth of information creates a poverty of attention." As for working memory, we do not work efficiently when it is saturated with information. Our memory is not unlimited.

Thus, we can perhaps better understand why the concept of the "digital native" is a technomyth. Not only are digital natives no more intelligent than digital immigrants, but the contrary may even be true. A study[18] published in the *British Journal of Educational Psychology* compared various cognitive parameters and concluded that an eleven-year-old child's intellectual maturity was equivalent to that of an eight- or nine-year-old child just 30 years earlier! We will have to examine how neuromyths, screens, and multitasking have contributed to this.

In 2009, Clifford Nass, the founder and director of the Communication Between Humans and Interactive Media Lab

---

[18] Shayer, M., Ginsburg, D., & Coe, R. (2007). Thirty years on a large anti-Flynn effect? The Piagetian test volume and heaviness norms 1975-2003. *British Journal of Educational Psychology, 77*, 25–41.

of Stanford University (the laboratory that performed the above-mentioned study on multitasking), declared, "It's very troubling [...] we have not yet found something that [multitaskers are] definitely better at than people who don't multitask," adding, "There's denial [about the results], but there's no surprise."[19]

There is no surprise because we have known for decades that true multitasking is no more than a popular belief; a myth. In fact, studies have long been speaking of the cognitive cost of multitasking.[20]

One alarming conclusion this world expert on multitasking makes is that ***"[media multitaskers] are suckers for irrelevancy."*** Media multitasking therefore ensures that when they are online, people forget the reason why they are doing what they are doing, and become passive and distracted.

But what are the underlying beliefs that have allowed these technomyths to fool us? The truth is that technomyths are in turn founded on *neuromyths*.

---

[19] Interview: Clifford Nass. (2010, February 2). *Frontline*. Retrieved from https://www.pbs.org/wgbh/pages/frontline/digitalnation/interviews/nass.html; Gorlick, A. (2009, August 24). Media multitaskers pay mental price, Stanford study shows. *Stanford News*. Retrieved from https://news.stanford.edu/news/2009/august24/multitask-research-study-082409.html

[20] Bowman, L.L., Levine, L.E., Waite, B.M., & Gendron, M. (2010). Can students really multitask? An experimental study of instant messaging while reading. *Computers and Education, 54*(4), 927–931; Cain, M.S., Leonard, J.A., Gabrieli, J.D.E., & Finn, A.S. (2016). Media multitasking in adolescence. *Psychonomic Bulletin & Review, 23*(6), 1932–1941; Uncapher, M.R., Thieu, M.K., & Wagner, A.D. (2016). Media multitasking and memory: Differences in working memory and long-term memory. *Psychonomic Bulletin & Review, 23*(2), 483–490; Uncapher, M.R., & Wagner, A.D. (2018). Minds and brains of media multitaskers: Current findings and future directions. *Proceedings of the National Academy of Sciences of the United States of America, 115*(40), 9889–9896.

Chapter 2
Neuromyths Harnessed by the Tech Industry

It is easier to break down an atom than a prejudice.
Albert Einstein
Ignorance is closer to the truth than prejudice.
Denis Diderot, French philosopher

In the last several years, we have seen the number of so-called "smart" apps and devices multiply. These are supposed to increase the cognitive abilities of our young children tenfold, and the companies that commercialize these tools tell us that we must use them to stimulate our children from the time they are very young, when 80% of the connections in their brain are formed. They tell us that our children have infinite potential, of which we should take full advantage during the propitious first three years of their life. They tell us further that these apps adjust to our children's learning styles and that they contribute to the development of each hemisphere of their brains.

They sell us digital products "designed in light of the latest studies," aimed at improving the learning curve of our young ones. Further, these companies tell us that our children are digital natives, which is why their brain is better able to multitask than ours. Hence, we should not be afraid of them doing multiple things at once while using technology. On the contrary, rather than forbidding it or worrying about it, we should encourage this practice, because the children of the digital age represent the "next step in evolution."

However, what many people fail to realize is that this sales pitch, which is the very reason for the proliferation of digital products (both devices and applications), has no pedagogical or scientific basis. If these products sell so well, it is in part thanks to the entrenchment of neuromyths in the world of education, both at school and at home. But what is a neuromyth?

21

The term *neuromyth* was coined in 1980 by the neurosurgeon Alan Crockard. It refers to pseudo-scientific ideas about the brain in medical culture. In 2002, the Organisation for Economic Co-operation and Development (OECD) warned against neuromyths, characterizing them as misconceptions about brain research and its application to education and learning.

These false interpretations are of course found in popular literature or in the media (news, educational brochures, personal development guides, blogs, books, education conferences with speakers who have no neuroscientific background, etc.). They appear in full force in the education world, presenting false premises that are then used to develop educational methods with no scientific grounding, which generates an ever-greater demand for supposedly educational products (DVDs to help with word acquisition, applications to improve memory, etc.). Among these many myths, are the following:

- *Children have unlimited intelligence*

- *People only use 10% of their brain capacity*

- *Each hemisphere is responsible for a different learning style*

- *An enriched environment improves the brain's ability to learn*

- *The first three years of life are critical for learning*

Let us address each of these myths in turn, as well as the grain of truth that lies behind each of them.

"Children have unlimited intelligence" and "People only use 10% of their brain capacity"

> *We have been endowed with just enough intelligence to be able to see clearly just how utterly inadequate that intelligence is when confronted with what exists.*
> Albert Einstein

> *It is inhuman that man dreams inexorably of a perfect humanity.*
> Jacinto Benavente, Spanish playwright

One of the neuromyths outlined by the OECD is that "we only use 10% of our brain." Do our children only use a small part of their brain? Do they have unlimited intelligence? Whatever the case may be, these two preconceptions contradict each other. How can we calculate 10% of what is infinite?

According to these myths, human beings have latent occult abilities, a sort of power, like those seen in the film *Lucy*, where the heroine is able to use an increasingly large percentage of her brain capacity, allowing her to, among other things, learn Chinese and communicate telepathically.

We now know that it is false that human beings only use part of their brain. According to Barry Gordon, a professor of cognitive neuroscience at the John Hopkins School of Medicine, the myth that we only utilize a fraction of our brain is a laughable falsity. In fact, Gordon, whose research has focused on the identification and implementation of methods aiming to improve language, memory, thought, and learning, asserts that "we use virtually every part of the brain, and [most of] the brain is active almost all the time."[21]

If our brains had an unlimited capacity, we would not be human. We would be more like gods. Indeed, the rapid diffusion and success of this myth could be, to a certain extent, the consequence of our vanity and difficulty with recognizing our limits as human beings. As Aldous Huxley said, "An unexciting truth may be eclipsed by a thrilling falsehood." Our imperfection is an unexciting truth. Perhaps this is why we have recourse to touching and comforting falsities.

What is most concerning is that this baseless neuromyth has spread like wildfire in the education world. In 2014, a study published in the journal *Nature Reviews Neuroscience*[22] revealed that 48% of teachers in the United Kingdom (and 46% in the Netherlands, 50% in Turkey, 43% in Greece, and 59% in China)

[21] Boyd, R. (2008, February 7). Do people only use 10% of their brains? *Scientific American*. https://www.scientificamerican.com/article/do-people-only-use-10-percent-of-their-brains/

[22] Howard-Jones, P.A. (2014). Neuroscience and education: Myths and message. *Nature Reviews Neuroscience, 15*, 817–824.

believe this myth. The marketing divisions of numerous hardware and software solutions companies have picked up on this in an effort to convince parents to buy their "brain games" for the sake of their children's cognitive development. Based on this neuromyth, we encourage our children to "have fun while learning" on the tablet, thinking that educational games will stimulate and increase their intelligence. We end up concluding, "the more, the better," because we confuse "more stimuli" and "more information" with "more intelligence."

Now, not only does our intelligence have its limits, but so does our memory. In fact, the scientific literature on the limits of memory is extensive.[23]

Human beings do not have infinitely flexible mental capacities. Our limits are obvious and we cannot reduce the pursuit of perfection to a series of techniques for developing supposedly "extraordinary" intellectual abilities, in order to use a hidden part of our brain that, in reality, does not exist.

"Each hemisphere is responsible for a different learning style"

Another myth mentioned by the OECD, also lacking scientific foundation, is the theory of brain dominance. According to this myth, children have a tendency to use one half of the brain more than the other, which has an impact on their learning style or personality. How many educational books and how many methods and "educational" apps have been sold thanks to this myth!

According to this myth, those who primarily use their right hemisphere are more creative and artistic, while those who primarily use the left are more logical and analytical. Although certain activities rely more on one hemisphere than the other (as is the case with language, which tends to develop in the left side of the brain, while attention is located in the right side), this belief has been debunked by studies showing that different parts

---

[23] Cowan, N. (2001). The magical number 4 in short-term memory: A reconsideration of mental storage capacity. *Behavioral and Brain Sciences, 24*(1), 87–114.

of the brain work together. Studies that have analyzed learning have found that there is always brain activity in both hemispheres, because they communicate with each other. What is more, *there is no proof of any sort of brain dominance that would have an effect on each person's learning style.*

Jeff Anderson, a professor of neuroradiology at the University of Utah and the director of a study[24] on over a thousand people between the ages of 7 and 29, notes that "The neuroscience community has never accepted the idea of 'left-dominant' or 'right-dominant' personality types. Lesion studies don't support it, and the truth is that it would be highly inefficient for one half of the brain to consistently be more active than the other."[25]

In 2006, the academic journal *Nature Reviews Neuroscience* published an article entitled "Neuroscience and Education: From Research to Practice,"[26] in which the author, Usha Goswami, an education professor and director of the Centre for Neuroscience in Education at the University of Cambridge, writes:

> At a recent conference held to mark the launch of the Centre for Neuroscience in Education at the University of Cambridge, teachers reported receiving more than 70 mailshots a year encouraging them to attend courses on brain-based learning. [...] These courses suggest, for example, that children should be identified as either 'left-brained' or 'right-brained' learners, because individuals

---

[24] Nielsen, J.A., Zielinski, B.A., Ferguson, M.A., Lainhart, J.E., & Anderson, J. S. (2013). An evaluation of the left-brain vs. right-brain hypothesis with resting state functional connectivity magnetic resonance imaging. *PLoS ONE, 8*(8), e71275.

[25] Novotney, A. (2013, November 16). Despite what you've been told, you aren't "left-brained" or "right-brained". *The Guardian.* https://www.theguardian.com/commentisfree/2013/nov/16/left-right-brain-distinction-myth

[26] Goswami, U. (2006). Neuroscience and education: From research to practice. *Nature Reviews Neuroscience, 7*, 406–413.

'prefer' one type of processing. […] Teachers are advised to ensure that their classroom practice is automatically 'left- and right-brain balanced' to avoid a mismatch between learner preference and learning experience. This neuromyth probably stems from an over-literal interpretation of hemispheric specialization.

A study published in the academic journal *Frontiers in Psychology*[27] reported that this myth is one of the most widely believed. For instance, 91% of teachers surveyed in the United Kingdom and 86% of those in the Netherlands believed that "Differences in hemispheric dominance (left brain, right brain) can help explain individual differences amongst learners."

"An enriched environment improves the brain's ability to learn" and "The first three years of life are critical for learning"

> *Less is more.*
> Ludwig Mies van der Rohe, considered one of the
> greatest masters of modern architecture

These two neuromyths are connected, which is why we are examining them together. In the article from *Nature Reviews Neuroscience*[28] quoted above, the author asserts:

> The current gulf between neuroscience and education is being filled by packages and programmes claiming to be based on brain science. The speed with which such packages have gained widespread currency in schools is astonishing. […] The critical period myth suggests that the child's brain will not work properly if it does not receive the right amount of stimulation at the right time. […] Direct teaching of certain

---

[27] Dekker, S., Lee, N.C., Howard-Jones, P.A., & Jolles, J. (2012). Neuromyths in education: Prevalence and predictors of misconceptions among teachers. *Frontiers in Psychology, 3*, p. 429.

[28] Goswami, U. (2006). Neuroscience and education: From research to practice. *Nature Reviews Neuroscience, 7*, 406–413.

skills must occur during the critical period, or the window of opportunity to educate will be missed. The synaptogenesis myth promotes the idea that more will be learned if teaching is timed with periods of synaptogenesis [the process of synapse development in the brain].

Approximately 33% of teachers in the United Kingdom and 46% of those in the Netherlands believe that "There are critical periods in childhood after which certain things can no longer be learned."[29]

The main argument that leads to this mistaken conclusion is the plasticity of the brain during the first three years of a child's life. Neural plasticity is a fact; however, we now know that it continues throughout life, not just during one's early years. There can be periods with greater or lesser sensitivity (conducive to certain types of learning) during the first years of life, but they must nonetheless not be considered "critical," since it is not a question of windows that close after the age of 3. *It might in fact be easier for children to learn Chinese during their first year of life. The problem arises when we conclude that attending Chinese classes is better for a child's development than spending time with parents*, or that children can and should learn Chinese from a screen (we will see later that studies say the opposite). In short, the problem arises when society is convinced that learning Chinese is essential for the life of a child, overlooking one of the most essential aspects of his or her healthy development in early years: the affective dimension.

We now know that *what is vital for children's healthy development during the first years of their life is not the amount of information they are given, but rather how responsive their principal caregiver is to their basic needs, which contributes to the formation of a secure attachment.*

---

[29] Dekker, S., Lee, N.C., Howard-Jones, P.A., & Jolles, J. (2012). Neuromyths in education: Prevalence and predictors of misconceptions among teachers. *Frontiers in Psychology, 3*, p. 429.

Daniel Siegel, a professor of psychiatry at the University of California, Los Angeles, School of Medicine, states:

> There is no need to bombard infants or young children (or possibly anyone) with excessive sensory stimulation in hopes of "building better brains." This is an unfortunate misinterpretation of the neurobiological literature—that somehow "more is better." It just is not so. Parents and other caregivers can "relax" and stop worrying about providing huge amounts of sensory bombardment for their children. This synaptic overproduction during the early years of life has been proposed to allow for a likelihood that the brain will develop properly within the "average" environment that will supply the necessary minimal amount of sensory stimulation [...].

He adds:

> More important than excessive sensory stimulation in the early years of development, however, are the patterns of interaction between child and caregiver. Attachment research suggests that collaborative interpersonal interaction, not excessive sensory stimulation, can be seen as the key to healthy development.

It consequently proves to be counterproductive to seat a child in front of a supposedly educational film or app in order to avoid "wasting a learning opportunity," when it has been established that, at a young age, it is important not to bombard children with information, but rather to strengthen their affective dimension.

How many times have these neuromyths contributed to stripping the role of parents of its meaning, leading parents to believe that they must overstimulate their children at any given moment, and that this task can be handed over to a screen? ***Neuromyths have certainly helped to distance many parents from their sensitivity and common sense in the exercise of their motherhood or fatherhood. We are not entertainers, we are parents.*** Interpersonal relationships give meaning to learning during childhood and a large portion of adolescence, because they shape our sense of identity. Screens should not be assuming this role.

The idea that a child learns largely by means of overstimulation leads to the media multitasking and digital native myths. Multitasking fosters passivity and inattention, and those who indulge in it lose their internal compass—or if they are very young, they struggle to develop one to begin with, lost in a universe of futile stimuli. They navigate at random, without knowing where they are going; the "why" (the goal or end) is replaced by the "how" (methods) or the "what" (instruments). They become dependent on external motivation and attracted by lights, sounds, novelty, rapid stimuli, etc. Their internal motor and their search for meaning are slowly extinguished. This process is not neutral from an educational point of view, because it profoundly affects the motivational structure of the human being.

Chapter 3
What Motivates Our Children

There is a driving force more powerful than steam, electricity and atomic energy: the will.
Albert Einstein

Some argue in favour of digital media use during childhood, claiming that it motivates children to learn. Many studies on EdTech (educational technology) solutions report an increase in engagement among students who use electronic devices. But what sort of motivation leads to this engagement? In order to answer this question, we must step back and pause for a moment in order to analyze the term "motivation." Motivation is a very complex topic. As complex as the human being. And this is not only true for the world of education, but also in family, work, and political environments, among others. In short, in life in general.

How we handle the question of motivation and engagement in the education system depends on our conception of the human being. To better understand this, we will outline three models of motivation.

External motivation[30]

Give me a dozen healthy infants, well-formed, and my own specified world to bring them up in and I'll guarantee to take any one at random and train him to become any type of specialist I might select [...].
John Watson, founder of behaviourism

---

[30] In the field of psychology, the terms "extrinsic" and "intrinsic" are used. Here, the author refers to the same concepts, but using more accessible terminology.

Some people think that children are exclusively motivated by external stimuli. This belief comes to us from behaviourism. According to this school of thought, everything is programable, and the voluntary aspect is not relevant, because children are completely dependent on their environment for learning. Also according to this mechanistic theory, children are mere empty boxes needing to be filled. Education is consequently reduced to a "training in habits" (a simple mechanical repetition of various actions), or, as bemoaned by Daniel Siegel, a "sensory bombardment." The paradigm of "the more, the better" fits perfectly within the behaviourist theory which has been—and continues to be—fertile ground for the neuromyths enumerated in the previous chapter. Behaviourism emphasizes the accumulation of decontextualized information, external behaviour (mechanical skills and habits), and visible emotional and physical responses, as opposed to internal mental states (such as motivations for acting). Behaviourism does not acknowledge the relevance of a person's inner world, or simply does not acknowledge interiority at all.

Behaviourism is founded on the idea that children do not desire to learn on their own, and hence that this desire must be inculcated into them from outside, by means of punishments and rewards. This theory does not admit the possibility that there is a natural desire for the good, the true, and the beautiful. This educational approach resembles the one used to train show dolphins in an aquarium. When the dolphins perform their act successfully, they receive a reward, like anchovies, or otherwise a punishment, like hunger. Rather than an educational approach, these methods inspired by behaviourism amount to little more than technical training for children. In short, behaviourism assumes and leads to *external* motivation, which causes children to become dependent on external sources for learning. But as soon as the motivating factor is withdrawn, children alternate between a state of boredom and anxiety, and feel "unengaged" and "unmotivated." This type of motivation fosters dependence and a deep apathy in children, because it does not awaken any internal desire in them beyond immediate rewards.

An educational milieu that privileges external motivation "produces" adolescents and adults who act solely in their own interests, which are generally reduced to the satisfaction of their immediate base instincts. They do things because they are asked to do them, and only to the extent that they receive something in return (money, compensation, favour, recognition, pleasure, etc.). In a society where people are moved by external motivations, everything has a price and every action is tallied. Thus, rather than exercising compassion, we speak of tolerance. Rather than giving generously, we offer the bare minimum. Ethics are reduced to strict legalism.

External motivation is a short-term solution. Those who claim to teach but do not inspire in their children the desire to learn are attempting to forge cold metal.

Internal motivation

> *The joy of learning is as indispensable for the student as breathing is for the runner.*
> Simone Weil

From the perspective of internal motivation, children's behaviour is not simply the product of automatic responses to rewards and punishments. Internal motivation arises from a desire to learn, to surpass oneself. Children are motivated by curiosity, a sense of responsibility, or a feeling of accomplishment.

33

Internal motivation causes children to act by and for themselves, without there necessarily being a material or external reward associated with the task at hand. The satisfaction or pleasure produced as a result of performing a task flawlessly, assuming one's responsibilities, or learning something new, is sufficient. To this end, this position maintains that children can and must be the chief protagonists of their education.

In the context of an activity, this paradigm is associated with the pursuit of personal growth. But although this model is an obvious improvement over the previous one, it is insufficient, as it in no way excludes selfish behaviour. The reality is that, under this model, children act for themselves and not necessarily for others.

Altruistic motivation

> *To him that knows not the port to which he is bound, no wind can be favourable.*
>
> Aristotle
>
> *Building a boat isn't about weaving canvas, forging nails, or reading the stars, but rather imparting a taste for the sea [...].*
>
> Antoine de Saint-Exupéry, author of *The Little Prince*

Altruistic motivation is built on the basis of internal motivation and refers to the motivation to serve, to give to others. *When children have an altruistic motivation, they do not do things only for themselves, but also reflect on the motives behind their actions and the consequences they will have for other people.* It is an *altruistic* motivation because it gives rise to motives that go beyond the individual. These motives give meaning to a child's actions.

The three motivational levers that we have just described are linked to an important concept in psychology: the *locus of control* (*locus* is the Latin word for "place"). In psychology, this refers to a person's perception of where the control of his or her behaviour originates (either externally or internally).

On one hand, those who have an internal locus of control attach importance to effort and responsibility, because they know that these can have a positive effect on their own actions and on what they control. ***Through play*** (which is not the same thing as the *entertainment* offered by the games one "plays" on a computer), **children learn to develop an internal locus of control.** They understand that their actions have an effect on them and on other people. To play is to actively prepare oneself for the unexpected, rather than simply letting oneself passively drift along. As it happens, entrepreneurs tend to have an internal locus of control, because they must proactively seek out opportunities, which demands effort and work. A person will be inclined to make the necessary efforts to the extent that he or she knows they will have an impact. An internal locus of control is associated with an internal motivation. Those who have an internal locus of control act for themselves and do not rely on external circumstances. Obviously, we do not control everything (illness, death, etc.), but we can influence many different situations, and ultimately, we can also control the attitude that we adopt in the face of events that are beyond our control.

On the other hand*, those who have an external locus of control tend not to assume responsibility for their actions, because they believe that these are dictated by their environment*, or that they are the consequences of other people's actions. Such people systematically shift the blame onto others. Thus, university students who have an external locus of control tend to see their poor results as unrelated to their actions ("my professor failed me") rather than seeing them in light of their own choices ("I failed because I didn't study enough" or "I don't understand the material," etc.). Rather than recognizing their mistakes, children with an external locus of control will fail to assume responsibility for their mistakes. At work, individuals will avoid making decisions for fear of facing the consequences, and when they are forced to make them, they will always seek the approval of their supervisors in order to avoid taking the blame themselves. People with an external locus of control will be limited to positions that do not entail many responsibilities—or even any—or to accepting leadership roles without really assuming the responsibilities and often casting the blame on others. People with an external locus of control are conformists, because they do not believe themselves capable of conditioning their own behaviour, and hence act like others, deeming it socially risky to stand out from the crowd. Conformity is not an attitude that favours creativity, originality, or innovation, except to the extent that the majority seek innovation. In this case, conformists will seek innovation within the confines of what is "in vogue," thus giving rise to plagiarism and imitation. Conformist children try to blend in without reflecting on the consequences or meaning of the actions they perform or leave off doing. They would rather commit a thousand wrongs than be a whistleblower.

We said above that altruistic and internal motivations are what give meaning to a child's actions. But what does this meaning consist in and why must it be the motor of education?

Chapter 4
The Search for Meaning

The secret of human existence lies not only in living, but in knowing what to live for.
Fyodor Dostoevsky, *The Brothers Karamazov*

The search for meaning is at the heart of the education question. The importance of "meaningful learning" is, in fact, a well-known educational principle.

You can attempt to explain to a child that 2 + 2 is 5, but in vain. The child can memorize it, but will never understand it, because it is false. As Isaac Newton said, "A man may imagine things that are false, but he can only understand things that are true, for if the things be false, the apprehension of them is not understanding."[31] What causes children to focus their attention on something is the meaning that it has for them. Children are eager for meaning; they need it. This is what leads them to take interest in their surroundings; to want to learn.

An education that does not answer a child's "why" is not an education; it is rather an absurd training fed by external motivations. Thus, George Lowthian Trevelyan rightly said that, "Thanks to education, a vast number of people know how to read, but do not know what is worth reading." **We lose ourselves in a sort of pedagogical activism that causes the means to become the goal and the end.**

In education, it is the purpose or the *raison d'être* of learning that gives meaning to education. So, what is the purpose of education? Immanuel Kant said that "Education is the development in the individual of all the perfection of which he

---

[31] Newton, I. (1950). *Theological Manuscripts.* (H. McLachlan, Ed.). Liverpool: University Press, p. 127.

is capable." For Plato, the goal of a good education is "to give to the body and to the soul all the beauty and all the perfection of which they are capable."

But what *is* the perfection in question and in what does it consist? Does it mean being a genius? Being good at everything? Not quite.

According to Aristotle, perfection is what has attained its end; what is complete. Antoine de Saint-Exupéry said that "Perfection is achieved, not when there is nothing more to add, but when there is nothing left to take away." These two definitions seem to contradict each other, yet they could also mean the same thing. According to the Aristotelian school, a thing is perfect to the extent that it possesses what it is able to possess, by virtue of its nature. No more, no less. To illustrate this, we can use the metaphor of a fruit tree. For the tree, perfection consists in growing, blossoming, and producing fruit. Of course, the environment (climate, soil quality, amount of water and light, etc.) must be favourable and can influence the tree's growth. Natural variation is also possible: the tree can extend its roots in many different directions, grow branches in a variety of patterns, and shelter birds of diverse species. However, the tree is what it is, marked by its nature; an apple tree cannot produce pears. And if we inundate its roots, we risk drowning it. In the same way, although our brain is endowed with a great deal of plasticity, which allows us to adapt to our environment, our environment cannot alter our nature.

Ultimately, education has meaning to the extent that it consists in going down a path that contemplates the perfection *of which our nature is capable*. Certain situations, however, involve pursuing a perfection which *our nature is not able to attain*, like, for example, teaching our children to read at the age of 1, making them do their homework while letting them play video games at the age of 12, or making them spend hours memorizing flashcards without actually understanding the material. As we saw earlier in reference to neuromyths, all the products that claim to "instill" in children a perfection that their nature cannot attain (for example, simultaneously doing multiple things that require information processing, bombarding them with information in order to increase their intelligence, leapfrogging over steps in their development, substituting human interaction with cold digital technology, etc.) and that deprive them of what that same nature demands (genuine interpersonal relationships, a secure attachment, contact with reality through sensory experiences) or that favorise external motivations, should not have their place in education. These products do not give meaning to learning, because they have no relationship to the end of education, to what is true and good for a child's nature.

Maria Montessori was one of the first to discover the ability of concentration in children, who are naturally driven to repeat the same activity, like going up and down the stairs, several times. Adults may not understand a child's logic, because their productive mentality interprets this action as being a waste of time. "Why are you going up if you just came down? And why are you going up again?" they will ask. In fact, children's logic reflects their nature. When children repeat the same movement or action, they acquire the perfection associated with this action and in doing so, perfect themselves.[32] They are not doing anything "productive," nor are they obeying an instruction in hopes of reward or from fear of punishment. They are engaging in self-perfection, thereby attaining the end of which they are capable, as Aristotle would say.

In this sense, the obsession in education with what is useful and productive, which manifests itself in meticulously planning and executing strategies to attain arbitrary objectives—like

---

[32] L'Ecuyer, C., & Murillo, J.I. (2020). Montessori's teleological approach to education and its implications. *Revista Española de Pedagogía, 78*(277), 499–517.

improving the ranking of one's school—often minimizes the importance of other areas of education that are considered useless, like the arts.

In education, the utility criterion can be a trap. Useful for what? For moving up in the rankings? And on what criteria are these rankings based? **To the extent that utility does not refer back to the raison d'être of education, it has no meaning.** Conversely, if something contributes to the perfection a child is able to attain, it is possible that it has meaning in itself, despite having no apparent utility.

Happiness and joy can also be traps when we consider them as ends in themselves. In reality, happiness is a state of fulfilment, which is a consequence, not a means or an end. Since becoming parents, how many conferences and seminars have we listened to, how many books stuffed full of ready-made recipes have we read, selling us the perfect formula for our children's happiness? Erich Fromm warned that "If you are not happy with everything you already have, you won't be happy either with everything that you don't have." Happiness is deeper and more meaningful than a strategic objective set by supposedly "perfect" families; it is the consequence of a full and meaningful life. If there is no meaning, there is no real happiness. When there is meaning, happiness is possible, despite suffering and difficulties.

Educational myths have alienated us from what is true, good, and beautiful for children. They have made us seek perfection where it cannot be found; they have stripped children of their internal motivations and prevented them from developing altruistic motivations. In some respects, children can, unconsciously, ask themselves the following question: What use is it to me to learn if the goal is to have an intelligence, a memory, that are beyond my capabilities? What good is it to learn if it does not allow me the possibility of being in harmony with what my inner nature demands? Thus, joy as a consequence of doing things well is a barometer that tells us if what a child is doing makes sense or not.

At the end of the day, educating in order to attain the perfection that is possible for the child means educating realistically. We cannot ask a bird to dive into the depths of the ocean or a daisy to grow on a tree. Thus, what is demanded by our nature marks out the itinerary of an education that makes sense; one that is truly meaningful.

On a few occasions, I asked why such-and-such was being done in certain schools and the response was: "I don't know, but it doesn't do any harm, does it?" We can therefore ask ourselves: What is the goal, the end of this activity or that methodology (besides the fact that it "doesn't do any harm")? **We must know that there is nothing neutral in education.** To the extent that a methodology serves an end that our nature is able to attain, it has meaning. The opposite would be meaningless.

Let us take discipline, for example. Discipline is meaningful only to the extent that it conforms to education's *raison d'être*. Yet it sometimes happens that this conformity is absent, particularly when we attach too much importance to something irrelevant, or do not pay enough attention to something that actually matters. For example, is it not strange that we fuss over five- or six-year-old children making noise or dirtying their pants as they play in the backyard or climb a tree? And is it not strange that just a few years later, we let them use the Internet without supervision; acquire a digital identity on social media; and share selfies taken in front of the bathroom mirror with the $900 smartphone that we gave them, without their really needing it?

In short, children are interested by whatever has meaning. This is the most noble motivation found in the human being. It is what allows us to be attentive and concentrate on a task for an extended period of time. By contrast, children without an internal compass who are constantly bombarded with rapid and noisy stimuli are candidates for inattention. We might wonder, then, "How is it possible that an inattentive child be so fascinated by a screen?" Fascination and attention are often, and mistakenly, confused.

Chapter 5
When Fascination Is Sold for Attention

The unhappy have no other need in the world than men able to give them their attention. Attention is the rarest and purest form of generosity.

Simone Weil, French philosopher

The attention that we give to something is the most precise barometer of our love for it.

Pablo d'Ors, Spanish priest and writer

Nowadays, whether in the personal, familial, or professional sphere, one of the rarest goods is attention. We persist in saying that time is the most precious commodity, but there is no less time today than there was yesterday. A day is 24 hours long—it always has been, and that will never change. We have no shortage of time to focus on what is important. However*, we have substituted the sustained attention that we once reserved for important things with a futile fascination with novelty.*

Fascination is a passive attitude towards frequent and intermittent stimuli. It is the attitude of someone who is controlled by external stimuli and is constantly on the lookout for new sensations in order to relieve his or her dependence on them.

Sustained attention, however, is a by-product of wonder and admiration. As explained in my previous book, *The Wonder Approach*, wonder is the very motor of learning. Thus, sustained attention is an active attitude of openness in the face of reality. It comes from within. As for fascination, it is above all passive, and does not lead to genuine motivation, but rather to the feeling of being engaged.

Furthermore, other important data make it possible to understand the difference between attention and fascination, particularly the fact that experts on attention-deficit/hyperactivity disorder (ADHD) make a distinction between an attention deficit displayed while a child is in front of a screen and one displayed in the real world. ADHD cannot be diagnosed in a child while he or she is watching a screen. Why? We have all seen that a child with an attention deficit can easily spend hours in front of a screen.

> *"Doctor, at school, they say our son has an attention deficit, but my son can focus on video games for hours at a time. I am certain there is nothing wrong with his attention span."*

This is what teachers might observe in classes outfitted with digital devices:

> *"With the introduction of tablets into our schools, we have fewer behavioural and motivational problems. Children pay attention in class; they don't take their eyes off the screen."*

There is an explanation for this. When overstimulated children are bored in class, there are two options. The first is to help them to adjust themselves to reality. The second consists in providing them with extraordinary artificial stimuli, like screens, whose novelty and format fascinate and captivate them. But this is a "Band-Aid" solution; that is to say, when the bandage is removed, we are confronted with the same educational challenges as before. Christopher Lucas, a doctor of child psychiatry at the University of New York, explains that the attention of a child in front of a screen is "not sustained attention in the absence of rewards. It's sustained attention with frequent intermittent rewards."[33] When children appear

---

[33] Klass, P. (2011, May 9). Fixated by screens, but seemingly nothing else. *The New York Times.* https://www.nytimes.com/2011/05/10/health/views/10klass.html

attentive in front of a screen, captured by this system of reward, it is not because they are exerting themselves, but rather because the locus of control is external. Consequently, this is not a good indicator of focused attention.

What mechanism is responsible for attention and what is at the origin of sustained attention?

In the scientific literature, the metaphor of a nightclub bouncer has been used to illustrate the role of attention. The bouncer represents attention; the nightclub, working memory.[34] Working memory is like a temporal warehouse where the information we receive is handled, while awaiting our attention. Studies reveal that sustained attention is essential for our working memory to function properly. Working memory has a crucial importance, to the point of being identified as a reliable indicator of academic success.[35] Even more than IQ! Attention is what enables us to filter and select relevant information.

Let us return to the metaphor. If the bouncer fails to make good decisions about who to let in, the nightclub (representing working memory) will before long be full. A congested working memory cannot function properly. The consequences that will follow include: learning difficulties and mistakes, the deterioration of the quality and depth of thought, the loss of a sense of relevancy, etc.

The conclusion? Presumably, the nightclub does not have an infinite amount of space. The same goes for our working memory, as we saw above. The working memory's capacity is limited, and thus we must be careful about the information we choose to let in. We must select not only in terms of quantity,

---

[34] Like any metaphor, this one is not perfect, as a person's working memory and attention work together, not separately. In addition, working memory is not, strictly speaking, a place of work.

[35] Alloway, T.P., & Alloway, R.G. (2010). Investigating the predictive roles of working memory and IQ in academic attainment. *Journal of Experimental Child Psychology, 106*(1), 20–29.

but also of quality. It is not therefore recommended that we set our children adrift on a sea of decontextualized information. We should at least avoid doing so before they are prepared to distinguish between what is true and what is false, between what is meaningful and what is not, and before they have the willpower to say no to what is dangled in front of them. But how many children and teenagers have the qualities that enable them to do so?

Before a sea of decontextualized information, their absent gaze shifts back and forth, they register snatches of insignificant information—information with no coherent narrative—and their sense of touch, deprived of human contact, is reduced to a single part of their body: their finger. The more fascinated they are, the less they look for meaning and the less they are motivated. On social media, lacking the ability to judge between what is pertinent and what is not, a young person who should normally be in search of meaning becomes passive and easily falls prey to fake news and irrelevancy.

"Suckers for irrelevancy," said the lead researcher of the Stanford study on multitasking[36] that we discussed earlier. By definition, what is irrelevant is devoid of meaning. What captures attention, on the other hand, is, precisely, meaning. One of the advantages of technology is that access to every sort of information is only a click away. But before clicking, we must train the bouncer to recognize what has meaning and what does not and to prioritize information, since our working memory is limited. It is not reasonable to claim that a child will be able to develop the ability to recognize what is meaningful with a tablet

---

[36] Interview: Clifford Nass. (2010, February 2). *Frontline.* Retrieved from https://www.pbs.org/wgbh/pages/frontline/digitalnation/interviews/na ss.html; Gorlick, A. (2009, August 24). Media multitaskers pay mental price, Stanford study shows. *Stanford News.* Retrieved from https://news.stanford.edu/news/2009/august24/multitask-research-study-082409.html.

in his or her hands. ***Knowing how to discern between what is relevant or not is not a mere technical ability. So, rather than speaking in terms of "digital competencies," we should instead speak in terms of the ability to understand something contextually.***

An understanding of the context is not acquired via an electronic device, but rather from a personalized education, imparted by another human being. It is a solid humanistic formation that will allow young learners to develop criteria of relevancy and meaning in order to make sense of the abundance of information available in the digital world. To this end, all the methods and tools (digital or otherwise) that only target the child's external motivation are not helpful, because they foment in them an attitude of passivity. Time is much better invested if we help a child exercise discernment:

> "Is it relevant or not? Why?"
>
> "What is beautiful? What is not?"
>
> "What is true? What is good?"
>
> "What does a sense of privacy mean? Why?"
>
> "What is the information that I am looking for at this exact moment? Why am I looking for this information?"
>
> "Who is important to me and who can I trust?"
>
> "What is an opinion, a fact, a trustworthy piece of information, and non-factual information? Why?"
>
> "Who am I?"

In the absence of self-control, a sense of privacy, aesthetic sensibility, the ability to filter what is relevant, as well as many other qualities and virtues, a child's "working memory bouncer" cannot keep up with the avalanche of information, music, and visual stimuli that screens present.

It is indispensable that children and teenagers answer all of these questions before entering a world that constantly solicits their attention. Let us return to the definition of education as a search for the perfection of which our nature is capable by making use of the metaphor of a crystal vase, which we have to fill with objects of various sizes, within the limits of its capacity. It is important to first fill the vase with the largest objects; the most important ones. Children must develop clear criteria of relevancy. Then, the medium-sized objects can be put in, followed by the smallest ones. At the very end, there will also be space to add water to the vase. If we start with the water and the small objects, it will be impossible to fit the larger ones in and the water will end up spilling everywhere. Thus, we can say that **the current educational crisis is, to a large extent, a crisis of attention. Children are stuffed full of fragmented information that prevents them from grasping the essential: the meaning.** We have acclimatized children to a pace that does not respect their internal rhythm; we have made them dependent on an overstimulation that extinguishes their desire to learn. Consequently, their attention is depleted and scattered.

Studies show that attention can be focused intentionally or that it can be absorbed by environmental stimuli. One study[37] published in *The Journal of Neuroscience* found that the ability to avoid distractions varies from one person to another. But what causes this disparity? The same study concluded that difficulty being attentive, associated with a low-capacity working memory, could be a consequence of a deficiency in the ability to filter out external information that we receive involuntarily and which distracts us. On the other hand, the study concluded that the ability to filter information on the basis of objectives

---

[37] Fukuda, K., & Vogel, E.K. (2009). Human variation in overriding attentional capture. *The Journal of Neuroscience, 29*(27), 8.726–8.733.

helps a person to manage attention well. Hence the importance of having clear objectives, and not simply letting oneself be passively carried along. Objectives are the big objects, those that must be placed in the metaphorical crystal vase before any of the others.

It was no accident that Isaac Newton attributed his discoveries "more to patient attention than to any other talent." Children cannot all be like Newton, and it should not be the goal of parents or the education system to make them all geniuses of his calibre. But let us imagine for a moment that one of our children has the talent to become, one day, a Nobel Prize winner. To treat education as a simple accumulation of encyclopedic knowledge and to invest in a technological arsenal that will transform them into "suckers for irrelevancy" could have the effect of preventing them from ever attaining that goal, or from even coming close. *We have the right to ask what would have become of Mozart, Picasso, Socrates, or Shakespeare if they had found themselves, at the age of 8, with a tablet in their hands.*

Chapter 6
The Invisible Hand in Our Homes

*In regard to propaganda the early advocates of universal literacy
and a free press envisaged only two possibilities: the propaganda
might be true, or it might be false. They did not foresee what in fact
has happened, above all in our Western capitalist democracies—the
development of a vast mass communications industry, concerned in
the main neither with the true nor the false, but with the unreal, the
more or less totally irrelevant. In a word, they failed to take into
account man's almost infinite appetite for distractions.*
Aldous Huxley, English writer and philosopher

According to a study cited above,[38] 53% of American children
have a smartphone by the age of 11 and 69% have one by the
age of 12. What drives us to purchase a phone for our children
at these ages?

In principle, all parents want the best for their children. No
one buys their children a tablet or smartphone thinking that it
will do them harm. We dare to hope that they will make good
use of these tools. We do it so that they might take advantage
of the opportunities for making new friends and have an
acceptable social life; so that they do not miss the boat on new
technologies; so that they might be technological innovators; so
that they can, above all, learn to use these devices responsibly;
so that they will not be the oddball in the class; or so that we
will be able to find them in unforeseen circumstances. Later on,
we will address all of these arguments.

It is well known that most children inherit their first phone
from a family member who has purchased a new one, or has

---

[38] Rideout, V., & Robb, M.B. (2019). The Common Sense census: Media
use by tweens and teens. San Francisco, CA: Common Sense Media.

been gifted one by his or her cell phone provider. In fact, who has not received a call from their phone provider and been presented with an attractive offer with the addition of a line for their son or daughter? Before we know it, we think "That's great! We'd be able to reach our child at any time." The promotion is generally accepted on the spot during a high-pressure sales pitch, and the decision is made without considering the consequences of offering a child access to the Internet at all times. The child starts with phone calls, Internet searches, using Wi-Fi while out and about, as young people so often do. We are then faced with the dilemma of whether or not to check our son or daughter's search history, but we decide not to do so in the end, for fear of being "bad parents." Whether we do it or not, we can surmise the risks…. And our child becomes more and more dependent, and we realize that this was not what we had expected at the start.

"We shouldn't have given him a smartphone. He spends all day on it…"

"It's too late; there's no choice except to trust him. It's impossible to go back at this point; we'd be fighting a losing battle."

Without realizing it, and convincing ourselves that we are being "good parents," we fall into our cell phone provider's commercial trap. What are these companies pursuing? The answer is within easy reach, in the annual report that all publicly traded companies release for their investors. In these documents, we can see the structure of each corporation's business model by means of a series of indicators: increase in share market; increase in client base; application downloads; consumption of paid content; time spent on phone calls, on text messaging, and online; etc. The growth of these indicators is indispensable for obtaining a good stock index, which makes financing the company possible, and ultimately ensures its financial sustainability. To this end, it is necessary for these companies to sell devices that fascinate and make their users dependent on them. As Steve Jobs said, "We made the buttons on the screen look so good you'll want to lick them." It is also necessary to develop applications and content that are addictive. The former president of Facebook, Sean Parker, has publicly acknowledged that the site was designed to exploit human vulnerability.[39] And *who are the users who become dependent most easily? Children and teenagers, without a doubt, because their minds are still relatively immature.*

What is more, content providers (of movies, music, news, apps, etc.) are less and less involved in the business of selling content. What does this mean? We are well acquainted with the claim that "*the media industry is not in the business of supplying content to its readers, but rather in the business of supplying readers to those who sponsor their content, namely, their advertisers*." It is precisely these advertising agencies who plaster screens with their brands and advertisements. In summary, all of these companies are in the business of finding sponsors—advertising agencies—for their content. The Internet is consequently a window for marketing. In a 1996 interview granted to *Wired*,[40] Steve Jobs noted that the real winners of the Web were not those who share but rather those who sell.

It is not a question here of imputing motives to companies. We already know that they do not have motives, because they are not flesh and blood. Companies follow an economic logic and their executives are at the service of this logic, especially if

---

[39] Solon, O. (2017, November 9). Ex-Facebook president Sean Parker: Site made to exploit human 'vulnerability'. *The Guardian*. https://www.theguardian.com/technology/2017/nov/09/facebook-sean-parker-vulnerability-brain-psychology

[40] Wolf, G. (1996, February 4). Steve Jobs: The next insanely great thing. *Wired*. https://www.wired.com/1996/02/jobs-2/

the companies are publicly traded, because then the executives are obliged to maximize short-term shareholder value. For this reason, there can be a sort of inconsistency between what executives personally believe—not allowing their children to use electronic devices when they are young, registering them in screen-free schools, etc.—and what their companies do: promoting the sale of devices (smartphones, tablets, etc.) that expose young people to inappropriate content, sponsoring companies that sell apps that exploit technomyths, in order to convince "good parents" to expose their children to the digital world as soon as possible, etc. Furthermore, it is this same industry that, under the banner of "social responsibility," sponsors a large percentage of the research on digital technologies and the majority of education congresses, pays the honorariums for the speakers at these events, and invests in advertising for its products in the media. Due to the fact that the business model of print media is almost a thing of the past, media outlets are now turning to other sources of revenue. An increasingly large percentage of the media's income comes from sponsorship and advertising by tech companies. As a result, the media is more likely to be reluctant to publish content that negatively impacts these corporations. *In an obvious conflict of interest, these companies disseminate favourable reviews of their products by means of the media, congresses, and studies, generating a favourable attitude towards their economic interests.* Thus, the sad view of economist Milton Friedman is realized: "The social responsibility of business is to increase its profits."

In practice, this is not always the case, because there are always business executives who consciously keep the common good in view—people who understand that businesses are important for the economic and social development of our society and who do not presume that there is any inherent contradiction in bringing in profits on one hand, while creating value for their customers and employees on the other. These executives understand that the key to their companies' sustainability lies in producing good results, while at the same time creating value for customers and treating employees, society, the environment, etc. in an ethical manner ("doing good and doing well").

However, Friedman's philosophy continues to inspire many companies. This mindset is absurd in the long term, because the pursuit of personal interests typical of this philosophy only produces external motivation in employees. This sort of motivation is not exactly the most productive in a company, because it is linked neither to loyalty nor commitment. We can therefore observe that it is not only our children and students who need an infusion of internal and altruistic motivation, but also the business world. The education system could serve as a transmission belt, allowing these motivations to transform the business sector into a world of greater solidarity, respect, and above all, responsibility, which can be compatible with companies seeking to make profit, but never at any cost whatsoever.

Friedman claimed that "the business of business is business," and that "a corporate executive is an employee of the owners of the business" whose responsibility is "to conduct the business in accordance with their desires, which generally will be to make as much money as possible while conforming to the basic rules of the society [...]." In other words, the end justifies the means, as long as the law is not broken. Which is to say that if my cell phone provider follows this sad business philosophy, it is not serving my interests as a parent, but is instead exclusively at the beck and call of its shareholders, meaning certain gentlemen in grey suits who work for a bank or an investment fund, and who play the stocks with the money of other gentlemen who spend their time smoking cigars in their slippers in London, or who sail in their private yachts somewhere in Switzerland or the Maldives. They, not our children, are the first to be interested in the addition of a cell phone to the family plan.

Ultimately, **we parents would do well to prevent the invisible hand of the market from conditioning our educational criteria.** We should take the reins when it comes to the question of using technology in our homes, taking into consideration the fact that the commercial logic we have just presented has a great influence on us, our children, and the entire world of education. In order to do this, we need real data, information, and facts. So, what do the experts think of screen use in early childhood? Let us take a look.

Chapter 7
Media and Young Minds: What the Experts Think

There is no data to substantiate the claim that young children need to learn to become comfortable with technology. [...] The fact that children like something, or parents think they do, does not mean that it is educational, or even good for them. Children like candy, too.

Susan Elizabeth Linn and Alvin Poussaint, American psychiatrists

A study conducted in the United Kingdom in 2018[41] on children under 5 revealed that the primary website they visited was CBeebies, where one can find content that, according to the website's portal, "helps pre-schoolers learn whilst they play fun games." In a report published by Common Sense Media,[42] only 38% of parents surveyed thought that the less children are exposed to screens at a young age, the better. On the other hand, many parents of technology-using children under 2 believed that this use contributed to their learning (66%), their creativity (48%), their social skills (42%), their ability to focus (46%), improving their behaviour (36%), and their physical activity (22%).

"I don't really like them being on the tablet, but at least they're using educational apps, so they're learning something."

But is it true that children learn from screens?

---

[41] Childwise. (2018). *Childwise Monitor pre-school report.*

[42] Common Sense Media. (2017). Fact sheet. The Common Sense census: Media use by kids age zero to eight. https://www.commonsensemedia.org/research/the-common-sense-census-media-use-by-kids-age-zero-to-eight-2017

In 2012, the National Association for the Education of Young Children issued a position statement regarding the developmentally appropriate and intentional use of technology in early childhood education. It considered the technology a tool to support social interactions, provide opportunities to decrease the digital divide, and individualize learning.[43] This position has had an influence on parents and teachers and tablets are increasingly becoming a mainstay in preschools: there has been a two-fold increase in early childhood educators' access to tablets, from 29% in 2012 to 55% in 2014.[44]

However, a report presented in 2009 by the Joan Ganz Cooney Center at Sesame Workshop, an entity whose mission is "to harness digital media technologies to advance children's learning," recognized that there is no theory of learning founded on EdTech solutions: "Currently, no widely accepted learning theory for mobile technologies has been established, hampering the effective assessment, pedagogy, and design of new applications for learning."[45] Furthermore, in 2018, two important Apple shareholders sent a formal letter to the company's executive board, in which they shared their concerns regarding the "unintentional negative consequences" of its products on the developing brains of its youngest users.[46]

[43] National Association for the Education of Young Children, & Fred Rogers Center for Early Learning and Children's Media at Saint Vincent College. (2012). Joint statement: Technology and interactive media as tools in early childhood programs serving children from birth through age 8.

[44] Blackwell, C., Wartella, E., Lauricella, A., & Robb, M. (2015). Technology in the lives of educators and early childhood programs: Trends in access, use, and professional development from 2012-2014. Evanston, IL.

[45] Shuler, C. (2009). *Pockets of potential: Using mobile technologies to promote children's learning*. New York, NY. https://joanganzcooneycenter.org/wp-content/uploads/2010/03/pockets_of_potential_1_.pdf

[46] JANA Partners, & CalSTRS. (2018). Letter from JANA Partners & CalSTRS to Apple. https://corpgov.law.harvard.edu/2018/01/19/joint-shareholder-letter-to-apple-inc

In light of this sometimes-contradictory information, parents and teachers of young children often wonder whether it is better to reduce screen time at an early age, or if they should instead take advantage of the possible learning benefits. Faced with this dilemma, it is worth asking: Does the evidence support the introduction of technology at an early age? What are the recommendations of pediatric associations in this regard?

The American Academy of Pediatrics (AAP) has issued several recommendations regarding the use of digital media in early childhood: in 1999,[47] in 2010,[48] in 2011,[49] and more recently, in 2016.[50] Its recommendations of 2010 and 2011 confirmed the previous one: *The AAP advised that children under 2 years of age not be exposed to any screens, considering that studies have demonstrated that they produce more negative than positive effects.* Similarly, the AAP noted that recent studies have been unable to produce evidence of educational benefits for children under the age of 2. There have been, however, many studies warning of the potential danger of screens for the health and development of children in this age group. For children over the age of 2, the AAP recommended limiting screen time to less than 2 hours per day, while still remaining attentive to the quality of content to which these children are exposed.

---

[47] American Academy of Pediatrics. (1999). Media education. *Pediatrics, 104*(2), 341–343.

[48] American Academy of Pediatrics. (2010). Policy statement—Media education. *Pediatrics, 126*(5), 1012–1017.

[49] American Academy of Pediatrics. (2011). Media use by children younger than 2 years. *Pediatrics, 128*(5), 1040–1045.

[50] American Academy of Pediatrics. (2016). Children and adolescents and digital media. *Pediatrics, 138*(5), e20162593; American Academy of Pediatrics. (2016). Media and young minds. *Pediatrics, 138*(5), e20162591.

In 2016, faced with the technological tsunami caused by the arrival of the tablet and the smartphone and seeing that consumption was soaring among minors, the AAP felt the need to update its position in light of recent literature. Despite the increasingly high consumption rate among children, it continued to discourage the use of screen media (other than communication tools like Skype or FaceTime) for children under 18 months. As for parents who insist on introducing technology to their children between the ages of 18 and 24 months, the AAP recommends that they use devices with their child and choose good-quality applications. Finally, the AAP decided to reduce the recommended consumption to less than 1 hour a day for children between 2 and 5 years old. Based on the available pediatric literature, the AAP's main arguments for these age groups are the following:

- Children primarily learn from human interactions and real sensory experiences, not from screens;
- Children need to interact with their primary caregivers and screen time reduces the number of opportunities for this;
- Children under 18 months who are exposed to screens may suffer from delayed language development;
- The evidence shows that the benefits associated with the use of technology before the age of 2 are insufficient to justify the accompanying risks;
- Children under 30 months old find it difficult to transfer new learning from a two-dimensional representation to three dimensions, i.e. from a screen to reality;
- There is no solid evidence documenting the benefits of early screen exposure.

In 2017, the Canadian Paediatric Society[51] presented its recommendations in light of the academic literature and likewise recommended that children under 2 years of age not be exposed to any screens, and that children between 2 and 5 years old be limited to no more than 1 hour of screen time per day.

Many studies have established a relationship between exposure to supposedly educational DVDs and a decrease in the vocabulary and cognitive development of babies.[52] A study presented to the Pediatric Academic Societies Meeting[53] not long ago suggested that heavy exposure to tablets and other mobile devices leads to risks of delayed language development in children. ***Young children do not learn languages or new words with the help of DVDs, however "educational" they might be.***[54] Several studies show that the *video deficit effect* amounts, as it were, to a reality deficit in screen learning, relative to real-life experiences.[55]

[51] Canadian Paediatric Society. (2017). Screen time and young children: Promoting health and development in a digital world. *Paediatrics & Child Health, 22*(8), 461–468.

[52] Zimmerman, F.J., Christakis, D.A., & Meltzoff, A.N. (2007). Associations between media viewing and language development in children under age 2 years. *The Journal of Pediatrics, 151*(4), 364–368; Chonchaiya, W., & Pruksananonda, C. (2008). Television viewing associates with delayed language development. *Acta Paediatrica, 97*(7), 977–982; Tomopoulos, S., Dreyer, B.P., Berkule, S., Fierman, A.H., Brockmeyer, C., & Mendelsohn, A.L. (2010). Infant media exposure and toddler development. *Archives of Pediatrics and Adolescent Medicine, 164*(12), 1.105–1.111.

[53] Martin, S.S., Black, L., & Alessio, L. (2017). Handheld screen time linked with speech delays in young children. In *Pediatric Academy Societies Meeting.* San Francisco, CA: PAS Press Office.

[54] Richert, R.A., Robb, M.B., Fender, J.G., & Wartella, E. (2010). Word learning from baby videos. *Archives of Pediatrics and Adolescent Medicine, 164*(4), 432–437; Kuhl, P.K., Tsao, F.M., & Liu, H.M. (2003). Foreign-language experience in infancy: Effects of short-term exposure and social interaction on phonetic learning. *Proceedings of the National Academy of Sciences of the United States of America, 100*(15), 9.096–9.101.

[55] Anderson, D.R., & Pempek, T.A. (2005). Television and very young children. *American Behavioral Scientist, 48*, 505–522.

Furthermore, one study linked screen use during the first three years of life to attentional problems by the age of 7.[56] Another, recent study seems to indicate a statistically significant relationship between frequent use of digital media and difficulty with attention-deficit/hyperactivity disorder (ADHD) in adolescents,[57] which could explain why the Mayo Clinic, a major hospital and research center in the United States, recommends limiting exposure to television or video games during the first five years of life, as a preventative measure for ADHD.[58]

What is more, some well-respected pediatricians went as far as issuing the message *Primum non nocere* ("first, do no harm"), a maxim attributed to Hippocrates and applied in the field of medicine, in order to raise awareness in the scientific community of the importance of discouraging screen use during early childhood.[59]

It is important to add that the limits outlined by the pediatric associations are not merely educational; they are public health recommendations. The time limits they recommend must therefore be considered an absolute maximum, not a standard of excellence to work towards.

It must however be noted that the AAP, in its 2016 recommendations, does not discourage communicating with

---

[56] Christakis, D.A., Zimmerman, F.J., DiGiuseppe, D.L., & McCarty, C.A. (2004). Early television exposure and subsequent attentional problems in children. *Pediatrics, 113*, 708–713.

[57] Ra, C.K., Cho, J., Stone, M.D., De La Cerda, J., Goldenson, N.I., Moroney, E., ... Leventhal, A.M. (2018). Association of digital media use with subsequent symptoms of attention-deficit/hyperactivity disorder among adolescents. *Journal of the American Medical Association, 320*(3), 255-63.

[58] Mayo Clinic. (2017). Attention-deficit/hyperactivity disorder (ADHD) in children – Symptoms & causes. https://www.mayoclinic.org/diseasesconditions/adhd/symptoms-causes/syc-20350889

[59] Christakis, D. A. (2010). Infant media viewing: First, do no harm. *Pediatric Annals, 39*(9), 578–582.

other people (grandparents, parents, siblings, teachers, etc.) via conference call (using FaceTime or Skype, or WhatsApp, for example). This exception extends to children of all ages, as long as there is a pre-existing secure attachment between the child and the person with whom he or she is interacting via video call. The exception, which was originally intended for children whose parents were serving abroad in the American Armed Forces, can conceivably be applied to circumstances like the COVID-19 pandemic, provided that the communication is carried out under adult supervision. This is not to say that young children should be attending classes conducted online, as children under the age of 6 primarily learn through sensorial experiences.

Young children need interpersonal relationships for the healthy development of their personality. Time spent in the virtual world is time snatched away from human experiences. The screen consequently becomes an obstacle to the formation of a secure attachment. This is why the question of digital technology use by children cannot be reduced to "Is it good?" or "Is it bad?" We must understand that when children sit in front of a screen, they cease to perform several activities, some of which might be necessary for their healthy development and could be of more value to them on a personal level. The technology issue cannot be reduced to "Don't do too much harm." We must ask ourselves about the impact for children's development.

Children need what is real. They also need a human education, because they learn through interactions with other humans, not through screens. They need the gaze of their parents and teachers in order to understand context.

By way of example, let us imagine a man entering a kindergarten classroom in order to repair a light fixture. He climbs onto a ladder and lets out an expletive as his tool slips from his hands. Where do the children look? Do they look at the tool? Do they look at the man? No. The children look at the face of their teacher, in order to interpret what has just happened. If the teacher takes it very seriously, they will take it seriously; if she frowns, indicating that such a thing should not be done, the children will arrive at the same conclusion; if she laughs, they will do the same (and will add another little word to their vocabulary). And when they get home, they will tell their parents the story, reproducing the attitude of their teacher. The parents and teachers of a child are the intermediaries between him or her and reality. They give meaning to learning. A screen cannot fulfill this role, because it cannot contextualize information for a child. Children receive what is on the screen, as it is, without a filter.

A study[60] published in *Pediatrics* showed a relationship between television consumption by five-year-old children and problems with attention and concentration at the age of 11. This study indicated that watching television can have harmful effects that can persist over time, rather than only affecting children during the period when they are viewing screens.

Thus, screens do not contribute to the healthy development of young children. The reality seems to be quite the opposite. Neuromyths and technomyths, fuelled by companies that commercialize these products designed for children, have distanced us from the reality of their learning.

---

[60] Landhuis, C.E., Poulton, R., Welch, D., & Hancox, R.J. (2007). Does childhood television viewing lead to attention problems in adolescence? Results from a prospective longitudinal study. *Pediatrics, 120*(3), 532–537.

Chapter 8
The Culture of Precaution

Since nearly all of what we are told about technology comes from its
proponents, be deeply skeptical of all the claims.
Jerry Mander, American author

We have just discussed the risks of screen exposure for children: decreased attention, increased impulsiveness, lower vocabulary, etc. But we have only been speaking of risks. Are these studies enough? Are these recommendations exaggerated? Are we presuming that a child (mine or yours) who uses technology *has* all these problems? Will every child who uses this technology be affected by these problems? If it is only a matter of risk, is that sufficient grounds to prohibit or regulate the companies that design or sell these kinds of devices?

It is one thing to discuss the inevitable consequences for a child who is a heavy and regular user of digital devices. It is another to understand the difference between a culture of recklessness and a culture of precaution.

Many of us may remember the *Challenger* disaster of 1986. A closer look at this tragedy will help to illustrate the difference between the two cultures just mentioned. *Challenger* exploded 73 seconds after take-off, before the horrified gaze of millions of Americans that watched the launch live on television. It was one of the worst accidents in the history of the space conquest. Seven people lost their lives, including one, Christa, who was not an astronaut, but an elementary teacher chosen to participate in an educational program that involved teaching

American children live from space. An "innovative" idea that had the goal of revitalizing public interest in education.

Soon afterward, a presidential commission was created in order to discover the causes of the explosion. The commission was composed of members of the American government and NASA, as well as individuals with close relationships to these institutions. There was only one independent member: Richard Feynman, winner of the Nobel Prize in Physics. The commission's report was criticized for its indulgence towards the interests of those who had called for the investigation. Some engineers who had participated in the preparatory tests of the mission knew that the explosion was not an unforeseeable accident, but that it was in fact the consequence of a great deal of grave negligence, which had been identified before take-off. These engineers attempted to bring this negligence to the commissioners' attention, but they were compelled to silence, ignored by the media, and one was even dismissed from his position. Years later, he revealed his side of the story in news reports that no longer make headlines. Robert Feynman's assessment of the facts can be read in a text that was relegated to "Appendix F" of the commission's report. But what really happened prior to the *Challenger* take-off?

The engineers had already cautioned that there was a risk of explosion, given the low dilatation capacity of the O-ring gaskets in conditions of extreme temperature change. Faced with forecasts of very low temperatures the day before take-off, they warned of the risk of explosion, requesting that the launch be delayed until a solution could be found for the O-rings.

What happened next was unheard of. The senior managers of NASA challenged the engineers who recommended against the launch to prove that the shuttle was going to explode. The engineers could provide evidence of the *risk* of the shuttle exploding, but they could not prove, beyond any reasonable doubt, that the shuttle was *going* to explode. In short, what NASA's managers did was no less than reverse the burden of proof. Why did they respond this way?

The government had not carried out a space mission in several years and it had been criticized by the press for this reason. The teacher was supposed to deliver classes from space; delaying the launch would make them fall on a weekend. Further, the subcontractor that fabricated the O-rings did not want to look bad in the eyes of NASA, NASA did not want to displease the government, and the government did not want to get bad press from its citizens. In short, political, social, and media expectations were high: there was a great deal of pressure to go through with the mission. The risks represented an obstacle and were embarrassing for all interested parties. The only "acceptable" outcome was reversing the burden of proof. In his contribution to the commission's report, Feynman goes further and says that NASA had systematically under-evaluated the risks and that the decision to include a teacher in the crew was made frivolously, all the more because the *Challenger* mission was not a commercial flight, but was rather experimental in nature. The risk evaluation of the disaster by NASA's managers contrasted sharply with the evaluation of the engineers. The senior managers had estimated the probability of disaster at 1 in 100,000 launches, whereas the engineers spoke in terms of 1 in 200 launches. This discrepancy was the logical consequence of a culture that only wanted to hear good and not bad news—those that improved NASA's and the government's reputations with the public—which hindered objective decision-making. Thus, Feynman wrote in the report:

> Let us make recommendations to ensure that NASA officials deal in a world of reality in understanding technological weaknesses and imperfections well enough to be actively

trying to eliminate them. [...] NASA owes it to the citizens from whom it asks support to be frank, honest, and informative, so that these citizens can make the wisest decisions for the use of their limited resources.

Let us return now to the question of technology use in childhood. In a study[61] that endeavoured to develop a learning model with respect to the use of digital applications, the authors observed:

> **Children are in the midst of a vast, unplanned experiment, surrounded by digital technologies that were not available but 5 years ago.** At the apex of this boom is the introduction of applications ("apps") for tablets and smartphones. However, there is simply not the time, money, or resources available to evaluate each app as it enters the market. Thus, "educational" apps—the number of which, as of January 2015, stood at 80,000 in Apple's App Store (Apple, 2015)—are largely unregulated and untested.

When we read about the history of *Challenger*, we can draw a parallel with the mass introduction of technology into the lives of children, and not because there is a risk of a certain electronic device exploding in their hands, but rather because the burden of proof of a large-scale experiment has been reversed. **Why are we not asking technology companies to prove the educational benefits of their products, as well as their harmlessness for our children's health?** We should then also be taking stock of the relative advantage of these benefits, in order to see if they outweigh the disadvantages or risks. But instead, those who call for caution and prudence (the "technophobes") are expected to prove the adverse effects. **But science is very expensive and slow, and technological**

---

[61] Hirsh-Pasek, K., Zosh, J.M., Golinkoff, R.M., Gray, J.H., Robb, M.B., & Kaufman, J. (2015). Putting education in "educational" apps. *Psychological Science in the Public Interest, 16*(1), 3–34.

obsolescence is very fast, meaning that evidence of benefits and disadvantages always comes too late. Thus, it will always appear when a given technology is obsolete and has been replaced by the next one. As a result, the technology industry does not see any use in testing for risks and benefits. And if it does, the harm will already have been done. Imagine the damage that would result if the pharmaceutical industry followed the same logic!

The reality is that we are at once the subject and object of science; we are at once judge of, and participant in, the research. The human being studies itself. Thus, is there not a risk of failing to be objective in the way we approach the research and respect the results? Perhaps this dilemma explains why, when it comes time to ask questions about risks that concern us, we have so much trouble being objective. It is difficult for us to believe the results of research, or to acknowledge them as a society when they entail major changes in our lifestyle or refute our opinions or greatest delusions. *What word describes someone who is ignorant or who does not want to know, but who, in spite of this, does not hesitate to act? Reckless. And when there are economic interests at play, everything becomes even hazier.*

Nobel Prize winner Feynman illustrated the disparity between scientific data and decision-making by those who manage economic resources. He concluded his portion of the report with an appeal to the culture of precaution: "For a successful technology, reality must take precedence over public relations, for nature cannot be fooled."

Unfortunately, as explained above, neuromyths and technomyths have considerably contributed to widening the disparity between scientific data and the decision-making of schools and governments.

Chapter 9
Can We Really Miss the Boat on Technology?

Novelty is a concept of commerce, not an aesthetic concept.
Eva Zeisel, industrial designer and ceramist

New technology is useful, but [...] it knows it'll be obsolete by lunchtime tomorrow, so it has no incentive to be anything else.
Tom Holt, British novelist

We often hear arguments like, "We can't let our children miss the boat on new technology," "It's the future," or, "If they're going to have a place in the world of tomorrow, there's no question that they need to be digitally literate," and so on.

I remember one day in the 1980s, when I was about 10. As I was taking the chairlift back to the top of the Le Relais ski hill, in Quebec, I watched the man sitting in front of me. He was speaking on a cell phone the size of a shoe. I was very impressed. It was the first time I had seen a cell phone. It was a flashy "first-generation" (1G) device, likely manufactured by Ericsson, and must have weighed a couple pounds. Having one was a cause for pride; it was a symbol of the avant-garde. Cell phones were not yet popular in the way we know them to be today.

The 1990s saw the emergence of the second generation of electronic devices (2G), and with it, their popularization.

With the turn of the century, we saw the advent of third-generation cell phones (3G), which popularized mobile access to the Internet. During that period, I had the opportunity to work for a publicly traded Canadian telecommunications company, giving me the chance to see the huge technological advances in this area with my own eyes. It was at this time that I became aware that the phenomenon of technological obsolescence was an integral part of the telecommunication sector's business model.

Nowadays, it is well known that the electronic devices we use daily have an increasingly shorter lifespan due to programmed obsolescence, whether technological, functional, or technical.[62] Technological obsolescence is when a piece of technology becomes outmoded as a result of another more recent or more advanced product arriving on the scene, which instills in buyers "the desire to own something a little newer, a little better, a little sooner," as described by Brooks Stevens, the pioneer of the concept of programmed obsolescence.[63] It is an inescapable fact, if we stop and think about it, that nothing is more ephemeral than a technological innovation: black and white television, the VCR, the bulky office computer, the first cellular phone, the DVD, the CD, the tablet, the laptop, the various smartphone models, etc. On the cutting edge of technology's constant evolution, we are witnessing the increasingly frequent release of ever more sophisticated models that render the old ones obsolete. New users are lured in by the constant offer of "state-of-the-art" models, which ensures companies sustainable profits, and allows them to acquire capital on the market in order to finance their activities and thereby ensure their survival. How right McLuhan was when he said that obsolescence never meant the end of anything, but rather the beginning! In the telecommunications sector, this is the business model that every initiate quickly understands.

---

[62] Slade, G. (2006). *Made to break: Technology and obsolescence in America*. Harvard University Press.

[63] Adamson, G. (2005). *Industrial strength design: How Brooks Stevens shaped your world*. The MIT Press.

In the early 2010s, the fourth generation of phones (4G) appeared, and at the time of writing, the fifth generation (5G) is being deployed. A new generation arrives on the scene about every decade. And if we think that the fifth-generation technology is the final and definitive version, we are mistaken. In 1909, a contributor to the *Scientific American* wrote, "That the automobile has practically reached the limit of its development is suggested by the fact that during the past year no improvements of a radical nature have been introduced."[64]

Having completed this historical overview, we can answer the following questions: Was it necessary to purchase the first-generation, shoe-sized Ericsson phone, in order to skillfully use later models? Is it necessary to master the use of a third-generation model in order to be able to use one from the fourth generation? Obviously, the answer is no. In fact, technology is increasingly easy to use. *If, in the past, you almost had to be a NASA engineer to figure out how to use a first-generation Ericsson phone, nowadays, technology is designed so that anyone can use it. It is the "Plug and Play" philosophy*, namely, designing ready-to-use devices, as described by the companies that sell them. *If a three-year-old child is able to familiarize him- or herself with a cell phone in half an hour, it is not because he or she is intelligent, it is because the engineer who designed it is brilliant.* Given this, does it make sense for our children to dedicate a considerable portion of their childhood and the greater part of their school years to "learning how to use technology"?

Sometimes we lose sight of this perspective, due to an almost religious adulation of technology, as explained by Pankaj Ghemawat, whom *The Economist* deemed one of the great thinkers in the field of administration. He calls this

---

[64] *Scientific American.* (1909, January 2).

technological fever "technotrances," by analogy with techno music, characterized by frequently repeated and seldom varied notes, and whose 128 to 150 beats per minute produce an effect on cerebral activity. These trances distance us from reality and result in a person entering an altered state of consciousness. This hypnotic fascination for technological change mesmerises us to the point that we view this change as being critical for and indicative of the future. We completely lose sight of the objective reality.

Technotrances have been present throughout human history. They are not a new phenomenon. Wernher von Braun, a German space engineer, asserted during the Second World War that, "By the year 2000 we will see the first baby born on the Moon." The explorer David Livingstone once claimed that the extension and use of railroads, steamships, and the telegraph, would break down nationalities.[65] However, a century later, and despite the advent of the Internet and the cell phone, 90% of calls, web traffic, and investments throughout the world occur on a local level.[66] This is the case because people need genuine interpersonal relationships. We need to be in harmony with reality and the human dimension.

These technotrances have promised more than once to "revolutionize education"—a promise that technology has not fulfilled to this day. In fact, in 1921, Thomas Edison predicted that "the motion picture is destined to revolutionize our educational system" and that "in a few years it will supplant largely, if not entirely, the use of textbooks." In 1945, William Levenson, director of the Cleveland public school board, said, "The time may come when a portable radio receiver will be as

[65] Livingstone, D. (2005). *The last journals of David Livingstone, in Central Africa, from 1865 to his death*. Cirencester, United Kingdom: The Echo Library.
[66] Ghemawat, P. (2011). *World 3.0: Global prosperity and how to achieve it*. Harvard Business Review Press.

common in the classroom as is the blackboard." In 1994, it was said that, "The use of videodiscs in classroom instruction is increasing every year and promises to revolutionize what will happen in the classroom of tomorrow."[67] We must therefore realize that a technotrance is no more than that: a trance.

Will our children miss the boat on digital technology if they do not devote every year of their childhood and education to it? At the current rate of technological obsolescence, there is probably a greater risk of the opposite happening. They will have wasted crucial and irreplaceable school years learning to use technologies that will undoubtedly be obsolete by the time they enter the workforce.

Now we can no doubt understand the reason why many senior executives of multinational tech companies send their own children to elite schools that pride themselves on not using technology in their classrooms.[68] As described in a *New York Times* article, *the children of a number of Silicon Valley executives have never performed a Google search. They write with pencil and paper and their teachers use a traditional blackboard.* There is not a single screen in their entire school, and the school also discourages screen use at home.

Mr. Eagle, who sends his children to one of these schools and who is a graduate in computer science now working in executive communications at Google, says in the same article:

> The idea that an app on an iPad can better teach my kids to read or do arithmetic, that's ridiculous. [...] Technology has

[67] Semrau, P., & Boyer, B.A. (1994). *Using interactive video in education.* Boston, MA: Allyn and Bacon.

[68] Richtel, M. (2011, October 22). A Silicon Valley school that doesn't compute. *The New York Times.* https://www.nytimes.com/2011/10/23/technology/at-waldorf-school-in-silicon-valley-technology-can-wait.html

its time and its place. [...] It's super easy. It's like learning to use toothpaste. At Google and all these places we make technology as brain-dead easy to use as possible. There's no reason why kids can't figure it out when they get older.

Is Mr. Eagle right? Are tablets and laptops really useful for learning at school? What do the studies say about this? What about the digital divide argument? Can children use technology responsibly? Is technology truly like any other learning tool, with no side effects? We will address all of these questions in the following four chapters.

Chapter 10
What We Have Been Told About the Digital Divide

The digital divide argument has long served as a basis for political decisions related to education, promoting universal access to technology in developing countries or among socioeconomically disadvantaged groups. It has been assumed that Internet access would help to bridge the social gap between students.

We take it for granted that access to the Internet or electronic devices at home would help improve students' academic performance and employment opportunities. Narrowing the digital divide would consequently correct social inequalities. But this belief has never been proven. A study[69] that analyzed the concept of the digital divide over a period of 5 years concluded that, while it is true that the concept has been used and continues to be used to justify the enactment of social and educational policies, a theoretical framework, conceptual definition, multidisciplinary approach, and qualitative and longitudinal research are lamentably absent.

The study's conclusion is supported by a 2015 OECD report, *Students, Computers and Learning*,[70] which observed that countries that have made considerable investments in new technologies in the field of education have not displayed a significant improvement in reading, mathematics, or science. Conversely, countries that have not made this sort of

---

[69] Van Dijk, J. A. G. M. (2006). Digital divide research, achievements and shortcomings. *Poetics, 34*(4-5), 221–235.

[70] Organisation for Economic Co-operation and Development. (2015). *Students, computers and learning: Making the connection.* Paris, France: OECD.

investment have seen rapid improvements in all parameters. The report concluded that technology does not help to close the digital divide that exists between privileged and disadvantaged students. But how is this possible?

The studies reveal that despite limited access to technology in disadvantaged homes, such households tend to use technology in a more abusive manner. According to a 2017 report by Common Sense Media,[71] children 8 years old and younger who belong to low-income households have a higher daily consumption (3 hours and 29 minutes per day on average) than those who belong to high-income households (1 hour and 50 mins per day). According to another more recent report[72] from the same organization, this trend is mirrored in children between the ages of 8 and 12 who belong to low-income households. These have a daily average consumption of 5 hours and 49 minutes, while the daily consumption of those in high-income households is 3 hours and 59 minutes. As for adolescents between the ages of 13 and 17, those from low-income households consume 8 hours and 7 minutes daily, compared to 6 hours and 49 minutes per day for those in wealthy households. Thus, it would appear that ***users who belong to socioeconomically disadvantaged groups use technology in a more abusive manner than other young people their age.***

It therefore seems that ***increased access to technology does not reduce, but rather increases the socioeconomic gap***. An article in *The New York Times* speaks of a "new digital divide" between families that are aware of the need to limit the

---

[71] Common Sense Media. (2017). Fact sheet. The Common sense census: Media use by kids age zero to eight. Exploring the digital divide. https://www.commonsensemedia.org/research/the-common-sense-census-media-use-by-kids-age-zero-to-eight-2017

[72] Rideout, V., & Robb, M. B. (2019). The Common Sense census: Media use by tweens and teens. San Francisco, CA: Common Sense Media.

use of digital technologies and are capable of doing so, and, on the other hand, those that are not.[73] Perhaps because these families are more vulnerable to technomyths. This article also explains that in Silicon Valley it is usually public schools that adopt the use of technology, while private schools, where most Silicon Valley executives send their children, do not use them. The article concludes that the digital divide is not what we expected. Another *New York Times* article describes how wealthy Silicon Valley parents are the first to reduce or even prohibit their children's access to technology, asking nannies to sign contracts forbidding phone use while babysitting their children.[74] It appears that these parents can afford to offer their children the luxury of human interaction.

---

[73] Bowles, N. (2018). The digital gap between rich and poor kids is not what we expected. *The New York Times.* https://www.nytimes.com/2018/10/26/style/digital-divide-screens-schools.html

[74] Bowles, N. (2018). Silicon Valley nannies are phone police for kids. *The New York Times.* https://www.nytimes.com/2018/10/26/style/silicon-valley-nannies.html

Chapter 11
Is Technology Really Neutral?

The idea that technology is neutral is itself not neutral. It ignores intrinsic dangers and puts blame solely on users.
Jerry Mander

Is technology really neutral? Here is what Marshall McLuhan, one of the founders of contemporary media studies, said about this belief: "Our conventional response to all media, namely that it is how they are used that counts, is the numb stance of the technological idiot."

There is no doubt that digital media shape the lives, worldview, and values of our children. No one can deny that their behaviour, their education, and ultimately, our entire culture, are influenced by what they see on screen. By way of evidence, an only thirty-second Super Bowl advertisement costs over two million dollars. Companies obviously see this expense as an investment; they would not waste such large sums if their air time did not have a direct and immediate impact on the perception and consumption of their brands and products.

Whether we like it or not, we cannot ignore the effect of technology on learning either, and still less the way that it is used throughout childhood. For the reasons outlined in the pediatric associations' recommendations, technology can never be neutral for children, because they are at a critical point in their development.

Technology cannot be neutral because of what the pediatric literature calls the *displacement effect*[75]: **When children use screens, they are not doing other things that could**

---

[75] Christakis, D. A. (2010). Infant media viewing: First, do no harm. *Pediatric Annals*, *39*(9), 578–582.

better contribute to their healthy development. In other words, since the time available to us is limited, children's screen time is unfortunately not devoted to other activities that are more appropriate for their development,[76] like sensory experiences, quality interactions with family members, free or semi-structured play, or reading.

For instance, it has been demonstrated that ***children who have extensive screen time are less likely to read than those who have very little.***[77] A report on physical activity published by ParticipACTION[78] shows an increase in inactivity in children and teenagers, and attributes a sedentary lifestyle and lack of proper sleep to an increase in screen exposure.

Besides the *displacement effect*, another factor could explain why the decline in reading habits coincides with an increase in technology use. An American study that investigated the relationship between these two trends[79] showed that there is a significant correlation between the time young people spend texting and an increased rate of inattention in relation to academic tasks, while there is a negative correlation between time spent reading and inattention. This could explain why activities that require attention, like reading, are becoming less

---

[76] Vandewater, E.A., Bickham, D.S., & Lee, J.H. (2006). Time well spent? Relating television use to children's free-time activities. *Pediatrics, 117*(2), e181–e191.

[77] Vandewater, E.A., Bickham, D.S., Lee, J.H., Cummings, H.M., Wartella, E.A., & Rideout, V.J. (2005). When the television is always on. *American Behavioral Scientist, 48*(5), 562–577.

[78] ParticipACTION. (2016). Les enfants canadiens sont-ils trop fatigués pour bouger ? *Le Bulletin de l'activité physique chez les jeunes de ParticipACTION 2016.* https://participaction.cdn.prismic.io/participaction%2Fae04c198-db2e-4eea-bf7d-a3f2ed885e15_participaction+-+bulletin+-+2016+-+complet.pdf

[79] Levine, L. E., Waite, B. M., & Bowman, L. L. (2007). Electronic media use, reading, and academic distractibility in college youth. *Cyberpsychology & Behavior, 10*(4).

popular among young people, whereas activities that involve media multitasking are on the rise. The characteristics favoured by one medium (reading on paper) do not correspond to the characteristics demanded by another (using digital media).

Over the next several years, we will have to keep a careful eye on the effects of continuous screen use by children in an educational context. And we will have to keep an eye on what adding 4 or 5 hours of screen time during class and while doing homework to the current 6 or 7 hours of exposure involves. Children are taking part in a large-scale experiment, of which their parents are not always informed. ***Certainly, the schools that make use of these tools do so with the best of intentions, but it would be a mistake to design an educational method on the basis of good intentions, rather than on evidence.*** "Good intentions" cannot be a free pass for disregarding evidence-based education.

In 1996, Steve Jobs said, "I used to think that technology could help education. I've probably spearheaded giving away more computer equipment to schools than anybody else on the planet. But I've had to come to the inevitable conclusion that the problem is not one that technology can hope to solve. What's wrong with education cannot be fixed with technology. No amount of technology will make a dent. [...] Historical precedent shows that we can turn out amazing human beings without technology. Precedent also shows that we can turn out very uninteresting human beings with technology."[80] On another occasion, he said, "I would trade all of my technology for an afternoon with Socrates."

Furthermore, Mark Zuckerberg, during one of the most notable events of his endless apology tour—his appearance before the United States' Congress—said that Facebook was

---

[80] Wolf, G. (1996, February 4). Steve Jobs: The next insanely great thing. *Wired*. https://www.wired.com/1996/02/jobs-2/.

created to be neutral, but "it's clear now that we didn't do enough to prevent its tools from being used for harm as well." The solution? In 2018, Facebook surprised its users with the announcement of the hiring of 20,000 "news credibility specialists," a strange sort of euphemism for "news report editors," to review our Facebook pages and eliminate content considered "unsafe to the community." A heavy blow from a platform that has always declared itself "neutral." How does it decide whether a post is safe or not? What criterion does it use? Supposedly, neutrality. The almighty neutrality of a company that attributes to itself sufficient infallibility to stamp content with the seal of the *nihil obstat*, content that is created and consumed by 2.6 billion users—no less than a third of the global population. No religion, no organization in the world currently has so many adepts susceptible to the influence of the unquestionable dogma of "neutrality." A dogma with so many holes in it that it is beginning to turn into a recurring nightmare for Zuckerberg.

If we thought that the impact of technology was neutral and depended solely on how we use it, it is because we are forgetting that these platforms are not free. When we use them, we have to pay a price. However, we are often not completely aware of this, in spite of all the consent and user agreements with fine print that we have signed with a tap of the finger. In the case of social media, we do not pay with money; we pay with ourselves and with our children. And not only by dedicating hours of our precious attention to it. It goes much deeper than that. Platforms that offer content on social networks, or that permit users to share it, are not in the business of delivering content for nothing to their users. As we said above, they are in the business of delivering users to those who sponsor their platforms and content, including third parties.

Thus, *the currency used by social networks is the user: it is you, or your son or daughter.*

The attention and private information of a user are precious goods that have never before been the object of such economic and political power. So much so, that, as we now know, a political consulting firm, Cambridge Analytica, made illicit use of the information of more than 50 million Facebook users, which may potentially have influenced the results of the American election and the Brexit referendum in the United Kingdom, thereby changing the course of the history of democracy. Not long after, Facebook admitted to the exchange of user data among at least 60 companies, including Apple, Amazon, Samsung, and Microsoft. Perhaps this is why the young founder of Facebook has his camera and microphone jack covered with opaque tape?[81]

Given all of this, how can somebody still defend the idea that these platforms are neutral? And furthermore, how can we argue that thirteen- or fourteen-year-old teenagers truly have the maturity necessary to consent to an activity with so many consequences? Can we speak of a responsible use of technology when still immature minds are in question?

---

[81] Olson, C. [topherolson]. (2016, June 21). 3 things about this photo of Zuck [Tweet with photograph]. Retrieved from https://twitter.com/topherolson/status/745294977064828929

Chapter 12
Can Children Use Screens Responsibly?

Only a virtuous people are capable of freedom.
Benjamin Franklin

A survey conducted by the magazine *Consumer Reports*[82] in 2011 led to the conclusion that 7.5 million Facebook users were less than 13 years old, and 5 million of them were less than 10. The same year that this survey was made, the CEO of Facebook, Zuckerberg, declared that he would like children under the age of 13 to use Facebook, because "my philosophy is that for education you need to start at a really, really young age."[83] While many countries have now placed age restrictions on social media access, a 2016 survey for CBBC Newsround[84] carried out in the UK concluded that more than three-quarters of children aged 10 to 12 have at least one social media account, despite not being legally old enough for it.

There is no body of evidence that shows a link between Facebook use and skills necessary for school. On the contrary, a study reported that the academic results of students who used Facebook were 20% lower than those of nonusers.[85] A 2020

[82] Consumer Reports. (2011). That Facebook friend might be 10 years old, and other troubling news. *Consumer Reports Magazine*.

[83] Magid, L. (2012, April 6). Letting children under 13 on Facebook could make them safer. *Forbes*. https://www.forbes.com/sites/larrymagid/2012/06/04/letting-children-under-13-on-facebook-could-make-them-safer/#26cbb4ec587f

[84] Coughlan, S. (2016, February 9). Safer Internet Day: Young ignore 'social media age limit'. *BBC News*. https://www.bbc.com/news/education-35524429

[85] Kirschner, P.A., & Karpinski, A.C. (2010). Facebook and academic performance. *Computers in Human Behavior, 26*(6), 1.237–1.245

study[86] found that excessive use of social networking sites causes students to become distracted, thereby affecting academic performance. What Zuckerberg fails to mention, and as the *Wall Street Journal* explains,[87] opening up Facebook to children allows the company to acquire market shares in the gaming industry, which makes it possible to ensure growth potential for its shareholders. The same logic applies to any social network targeted at the youngest in society.

Following the same line of thought, we often hear that it is possible, or even necessary, to teach our children to use digital media by giving them access to an electronic device and the Internet as soon as possible. In other words, following this line of thought, it is best to begin at as young an age as one can in order to learn how to use technology responsibly. The rationale is the following: the earlier children begin to use technology responsibly, the less they will expose themselves to dependency, inappropriate images, and other risks during adolescence.

And what of this belief? Does early exposure to digital technology reduce the risks associated with it? Can we even speak of "responsible" use by children? And by teenagers?

The American Academy of Child and Adolescent Psychiatry affirms that "The ability to 'click' from one area to another appeals to a child's natural impulsivity and curiosity and needs for immediate gratification or feedback."[88] We all know just how much these devices captivate children.

---

[86] Masood, A., Luqman, A, Feng, Y., & Ali, A. (2020). Adverse consequences of excessive social networking site use on academic performance: Explaining underlying mechanism from stress perspective. *Computers in Human Behavior, 113*.

[87] Troianovski, A., & Raice, S. (2012, June 4). Facebook explores giving kids access. *The Wall Street Journal.* https://www.wsj.com/articles/SB10001424052702303506404577444711741019238

[88] Academy of Child and Adolescent Psychiatry. (2015, October). Internet use in children. *Facts for Families, 59*.

In ten- to fourteen-year-old children, there is a maturation of the brain[89] that involves the reconfiguration of their motivation circuitry. It has been demonstrated that children in this age group naturally tend to seek new sensations continually, due to a greater production of dopamine in their brain. Consequently, *during this period, the search for novelty, for what is gratifying and attractive, leads these adolescents to assign more importance to rewards than to risks.* This is not necessarily a cause for concern; this mechanism should be seen as a "gift of nature." When these young people are in an environment that respects their nature and healthy development, dopamine can bear interesting fruits. Hence, someone who makes decisions without giving too much weight to the risks can prove more creative and innovative. This is why we say that young people will conquer the world. However, the risks inherent in the use of electronic devices and the Internet (sexual predation, sexting, inappropriate content, dependencies, etc.) can increase exponentially during this period. And in fact, studies confirm that adolescence is a period of increased vulnerability to dependencies.[90]

The solution we are given is always the same: "Filters can take care of everything!"

> *Person in charge of electronics in a school: "There's no reason to worry. Each tablet has a sort of mechanism that lets us know when kids visit unauthorized sites."*

> *Parent: "Is someone hired full-time to review the history of all the kids in the school every day and follow up on any incidents?"*
> *Person in charge of electronics: "No."*

---

[89] Laurence Steinberg's dual systems model.

[90] These studies are analyzed in: Chambers, R.A., Tayor, J.R., & Potenza, M.N. (2003). Developmental neurocircuitry of motivation in adolescence: A critical period of addiction vulnerability. *The American Journal of Psychiatry, 160*(6), 1.041–1.052.

Parent: "And this mechanism, does it let you know before the damage is done or after?"

Obviously, when filters are in place, they can reduce the risks for children. However, these filters have a collateral effect that is never talked about: they decrease parents' perception of the risks and thus give a false sense of security. Convinced that these filters are the solution, parents introduce digital technology earlier. They offer their children a smartphone and let them access the Internet in their bedrooms. Certainly, the filters lower the risks. We must recognize, however, that the risks are still higher for children who browse the Internet than for those who do not use it at all. ***Installing a filter on devices of young people who are not mature enough to manage their attention and natural desire for novelty amounts to beating the wind.*** This is all the more true given that a mobile device can connect to the Internet anywhere. The well-known hacker Kevin Mitnick stated, "Companies spend millions of dollars on firewalls, encryption, and secure access devices and it's money wasted because none of these measures address the weakest link in the security chain: the people who use, administer, operate and account for computer systems that contain protected information." Bruce Schneier, an American computer security expert, is of the same mind: "If you think technology can solve your security problems, then you don't understand the problems and you don't understand the technology." The Los Angeles school district learned this the hard way. After investing 1.3 billion dollars in providing each of its students with an iPad, 300 students successfully hacked the school district's security system and removed all the filters, within the space of a week.[91]

---

[91] Blume, H. (2013, September 25). LAUSD halts home use of iPads for students after devices hacked. *The Los Angeles Times.* https://www.latimes.com/local/lanow/la-me-ln-lausd-ipad-hack-

As incredible as it may seem, a study[92] on American youth between the ages of 12 and 18 showed that parental controls (rules, search history review, and filters) were not a differentiating factor between young people who consumed pornography and those who did not. The same study found a correlation between a high consumption of pornography and a lack of emotional bonding between young people and their parents. Strengthening real, quality interpersonal relationships is therefore essential and prerequisite to a child's entry into the digital world, as is acquiring various virtues, like self-control and temperance. These virtues lead to the acceptance of delayed gratification and to an awareness of the existence of limits. This moderation makes it possible to gauge the risks associated with the search for sensations. But how are these virtues acquired? They manifest themselves when we come in contact with reality. Reality makes it possible to place restraints on oneself.

A few years ago, I became aware of the existence of a very popular day camp in Spain, during which children traverse a "frustration circuit" (a track with a series of obstacles). Intrigued by this, I asked what it involved. I was told that parents were willing to pay for their children to experience frustration. I wondered, "Isn't life full of opportunities for learning how to manage frustration?" I then understood that children who have never been told "No" do not in fact know how to manage their frustration. Incapable of tolerating it, they become sensitive, capricious, and unable to handle waiting. These children find it difficult to be happy, because life involves its share of frustrations, difficulties, and suffering. It will also be difficult

---

20130925-story.html

[92] Ybarra, M.L., & Mitchell, K.J. (2005). Exposure to Internet pornography among children and adolescents: A national survey. *Cyberpsychology & Behavior, 8*(5), 473–486.

for them to achieve their goals, because it is essential to sacrifice certain things in order to procure greater ones.

Some of us may be familiar with the "marshmallow test" conducted at the University of Stanford between 1968 and 1970 on 653 four-year-old children. In the course of this experiment, children were left alone in a room, with a marshmallow in front of them. They were told that if they waited for the researcher to return before they ate it, they would get two instead of one. The amount of time children waited before eating the marshmallow was then measured and the factors associated with the ability to delay gratification were analysed. The researchers established that attentional control was the key to delaying gratification. A four-year-old child who could not stop looking at the marshmallow and who imagined him- or herself eating it ended up giving in. Conversely, children who were able to focus their attention in order to "resist the temptation" were able to wait longer. We might then ask ourselves about the effects of media multitasking on our children, since, as we have remarked, studies report that multitasking scatters attention and transforms students into "suckers for irrelevancy."

Years later, researchers studied[93] anew the behaviour of these children, now adults. They discovered that the four-year-old children who had resisted the longest before eating the marshmallow had, as adults, better academic results, better management of frustration and stress, as well as a greater ability to strategically focus their attention. In the group of adults who, as children, had successfully delayed gratification, drug

_____

[93] Shoda, Y., Mischel, W., & Peake, P.K. (1990). Predicting adolescent cognitive and self-regulatory competencies from preschool delay of gratification: Identifying diagnostic conditions. *Developmental Psychology, 26*(6), 978–986.

consumption was less frequent, especially with those children who were psychologically vulnerable.[94]

While there has been some controversy over this test, an American study published in 2011[95] in *Pediatrics* found, similarly, that 20 four-year-old children who watched 9 minutes of *SpongeBob* were able to wait significantly longer before eating a snack than the 40 other children who either watched the slower-paced *Caillou* or were left alone to draw a picture. Thus, ***there appears to be a relationship between the accelerated pace of a screen and difficulty accepting delayed gratification***.

So, does introducing digital media at an earlier age reduce the risks associated with their use? ***It is not likely that exposure to immediate, fast-paced content, or applications and games that have rewards associated with them, help our children to accept and manage delayed gratification. It seems that it does precisely the opposite.*** The "digital diet" argument (giving access to electronics, but putting in place rules that limit screen time) is not, therefore, the solution to all ills, since negative effects can readily be seen after just 9 minutes of screen time. It is unlikely that a child who has access to everything at the click of a button can develop this ability to delay gratification. In fact, an education in self-control and temperance begins in childhood: waiting one's turn to speak at the table during a family meal; taking care of toys, books, and clothing, in order to hand them down to younger siblings; listening to and keeping a friend's secret; planning the construction of a cardboard castle.... All of these activities

---

[94] Ayduk, O., Mendoza-Denton, R., Mischel, W., Downey, G., Peake, P., Rodriguez, M. (2000). Regulating the interpersonal self: Strategic self-regulation for coping with rejection sensitivity. *Journal of Personality and Social Psychology, 79*(5), 776–792.

[95] Lillard, A.S., & Peterson, J. (2011). The immediate impact of different types of television on young children's executive function. *Pediatrics, 128*(4), 644–649.

make it possible to develop patience, self-control and inhibition, temperance, attentional skills—all those qualities that allow a child to delay gratification and eventually use digital media responsibly. Of course, it is much easier for children to develop these qualities if they are in an environment that does not saturate their senses and whose pace and rhythm respect those of their inner world.

To claim that children should receive a digital device as soon as possible in order to learn to use technology responsibly is like saying that the best way to develop their spatial sense is to take them to a 450,000 sq. ft. shopping mall to play hide-and-seek on a Saturday afternoon. Or like asking them to get themselves a glass of water from a fire hydrant without getting wet. *The best preparation for the online world is offline, in the real world.* Children or teenagers who prove capable of self-control, moderation, or temperance, possess one of the keys to giving meaning to their actions: they know how to sacrifice something good in order to get something better. People who know *why* they do what they do have the motivation to act. For example, to be able to sacrifice a party with friends in order to be fresh and ready for a test the next day, university students need to have a clear idea of what this sacrifice involves. They must have a specific altruistic motivation (I want to become a skilled professional in order to be able to carry out my work for others), and not simply an external motivation (I am acting in order to receive a reward or avoid a punishment) or an internal one (I want to do this because I enjoy it).

Now it is perhaps easier to understand why *the inability to delay gratification is one of the primary factors influencing school dropouts.* When children and teenagers are unable to put off gratification, their freedom of choice is, in fact, an illusion, because they are simply not able to choose what

94

is good or give something up in order to get something better. Their will is so weakened by the need to satisfy desire in the short term that we cannot truly speak of a free and informed choice. The concept of freedom—which is the ability to choose what is good—is hence reduced to the option to choose from an infinite selection of possibilities. Being free then consists only in having more options at one's disposal without, however, wanting to commit to any of them. Teenagers who have grown up with this paradigm do not make commitments on the level of interpersonal relationships, although from their point of view, they feel very committed, because they respond in real time to every message they receive from their 400 friends on social media.

The locus of control (whether internal or external) and delayed gratification are crucial issues when it comes to early technology use. They help us understand who holds the reins in a video game, on social media, or while using an application, however educational it may be. For a still-immature mind, the locus of control is evidently external. Children are captivated by systems (the Internet, apps, video games, etc.) that bombard them with novelties, fast-paced images, and rewards (points, likes, captivating images, the feeling of winning, etc.) that come from external sources. It is the machine that holds the reins and not the child. *Tablets and phones "motivate" children, but it is an external motivation, because a child's locus of control is external.* As proof of this, there are many studies on technology use in class that report an improvement with regard to students' motivation or engagement. In these studies, the assessment of motivation is subjective (teachers report that students seem "more engaged"). However, no body of evidence exists to support a corresponding improvement in academic performance. This distinction is very important. In still-immature minds and in those that have not yet consolidated the capacity for self-control and developed an internal locus of control, digital media engage by means of the entertainment and new sensations they produce in a young person, but they do not provide motivation for learning, because they do not themselves generate internal or altruistic motivation, which are the key to learning that is personal (that begins from within) and genuine (that is meaningful).

Thus, we can ask ourselves whether it makes sense to speak of a "responsible" use of digital media at certain ages. Responsible use implies a certain responsibility on the part of the user. Children without the capacity for self-control or an internal locus of control have neither freedom nor responsibility; they are shackled, because they do not have the ability to choose or responsibly engage in what is appropriate for them. *As long as children have not yet developed the strength of will to delay gratification, and as long as devices and applications are designed to addict them, is it not somewhat preposterous to speak of a "responsible use"?* The idea of responsible use is another mirage created by numerous associations and foundations that, while nominally working for the protection of minors, work in reality under the aegis of telecommunications companies, ultimately beholden to the balance sheets of the latter. Whatever the case may be, the belief that there is link between the early introduction and responsible use of technology has certainly contributed to lowering the age of technology use and establishing, in the popular imagination, a connection between technology and education.

Chapter 13
Technology in the Classroom

I can only imagine how painful it must be for those hard-core advocates of more-technology-the-better who predicted the end of schooling years ago to see that public schools are still around.
Larry Cuban, Professor Emeritus of Education at
Stanford University

We have been using interactive whiteboards for a number of years now and there are schools where books have been replaced by screens. Tablets, laptops, and notebook or desktop computers, as well as educational apps, are all part of what are commonly called *educational technology* or *EdTech solutions*. Despite their ubiquity, such "solutions" are educational in name only. Many parents rightly have doubts and wonder about the advantages and disadvantages of using EdTech for learning. Parents who research information are overwhelmed with arguments in support of this digital revolution in schools, whereas there are few voices calling for prudence and responsibility vis-à-vis the mass digitization of classrooms.

Where is the evidence?

What is not often discussed is that, at the present moment, the evidence supporting the supposed benefits of EdTech solutions is insufficient. In a *New York Times* article, "In Classroom of Future, Stagnant Scores,"[96] Tom Vander Ark, a former executive director for education for the Bill and Melinda Gates

---

[96] Richtel, M. (2011, September 3). In classroom of future, stagnant scores. *The New York Times.* https://www.nytimes.com/2011/09/04/technology/technology-in-schools-faces-questions-on-value.html

Foundation and investor in educational technology companies, recognized (referring to positive effects of EdTech solutions) that "The data is pretty weak. It's very difficult when we're pressed to come up with convincing data." Since 2011, when this article was published, the situation has not changed.

In the same article, Larry Cuban, Professor Emeritus of Education at the University of Stanford, asserts that research does not justify investment in one-to-one laptop programs and other EdTech solutions. "There is insufficient evidence to spend that kind of money. Period, period, period," he said. "There is no body of evidence that shows a trend line." To date, there have only been occasional studies, and these do not show a favourable trend; most such studies are either financed by technology companies or lack scientific rigour: no control group, prejudices around the parameters being studied, subjective indicators ("preferred by teachers," "engage students"), etc.

Whatever the case may be, this lack of evidence has not prevented the introduction of EdTech solutions all around the world, because, as we explained above, the idea that technology companies must prove the merit of their products before introducing them into schools is not yet accepted as public opinion.

However, a 2015 study[97] on the impact of computers in the classroom, conducted on fifteen-year-old students from all OECD countries, makes it possible to dismantle the idea of a link between computer use and improved academic performance. The study concluded that:

> 1) computer use beyond the daily average in OECD countries leads to worse results;

---

[97] Organisation for Economic Co-operation and Development. (2015). *Students, computers and learning: Making the connection.* Paris: OECD.

2) countries where the Internet is used less for doing homework have better results in reading comprehension than in those countries where such Internet use is prevalent; and

3) the essential skills needed for online navigation can be acquired by means of analogue pedagogical tools.

The fact of the matter is that *the absence of scientific evidence for benefits linked to EdTech solutions ought to be a call for caution and responsibility on the part of schools*, which concretely involves:

1) remaining up-to-date on related trends brought to light by scientific studies, and more especially on the negative effects of technology use in education;

2) providing parents with information on the pros and cons, so that they can make a free and informed choice about whether or not to let their children participate in this large-scale "experiment";

3) giving parents the possibility of withdrawing their children from this experiment by offering a non-digital option; and, above all,

4) never accepting gifts—tablets, luxury meals, cruises—from technology companies that offer their products. The practice of giving gifts to teachers or principals has, by the way, raised an ethical and legal debate in the United States,[98] especially when the investments that result are made with public funds in public schools.

External motivation

---

[98] Richtel, M. (2011, November 4). Silicon Valley wows educators, and woos them. *The New York Times*. https://www.nytimes.com/2011/11/05/technology/apple-woos-educators-with-trips-to-silicon-valley.html

As we said earlier, there is one parameter that consistently returns positive results in the many studies on EdTech: the motivation of students (they are described as being "more engaged").

A teacher: "It works! Screens motivate students more and quieting them down works like magic!"

People then jump to the conclusion that "engaged" students produce better results. However, this theoretical improvement in academic performance has never been rigorously proved, as Larry Cuban notes, giving the following explanation in another *New York Times* article and on his blog[99]: "There is very little evidence that kids learn more, faster or better by using these machines. iPads are marvelous tools to engage kids, but then the novelty wears off and you get into hard-core issues of teaching and learning." According to him, there is also no evidence that this use increases opportunities for employment when these students enter the workforce. **The defenders of EdTech solutions confuse the novelty effect with students' long-term motivation to learn. But time passes and the novelty effect wears off.** Consequently, the hypothesis that student "engagement" produces better results in the long term remains no more than an unverified hypothesis.

What is the reason for the paradox of an "increase in engagement" but a "lack of academic improvement"? Why does motivation not entail improvement? In order to answer this question, it is important to revisit the theme of motivation. We said before that there are three degrees of motivation: external, internal, and altruistic. Normally, a mix of different motivations

---

[99] Hu, W. (2011, January 4). Math that moves: Schools embrace the iPad. *The New York Times*; Cuban, L. (2015, February 5); The lack of evidence-based practice: The case of classroom technology (part 1) [Blog post]. Retrieved from https://larrycuban.wordpress.com/2015/02/05/the-lack-of-evidence-based-practice-the-case-of-classroom-technology-part-1

can be found in every human being. To illustrate this, let us look at the simple example of a hypothetical school announcement:

> *"Our school will be organizing a food drive for disadvantaged families. The class that brings in the most food will win a soccer ball."*

Here we have an example of mixed motivations: the altruistic motivation to help the less fortunate, and an external motivation: a material reward. Is it good to have mixed motivations? Many parents believe that it is, because "it all adds up."

In a multi-year study[100] conducted on 10,000 American students, a group of students with mixed motivations—internal and external—was compared to a group with primarily internal motivation. The researchers' question was: Is it preferable to have multiple motivations—internal and external? The study concluded that motivations do not add up together, and in fact compete with each other. The researchers noticed better results in the second group, namely, those who had primarily internal motivations, than in the group of students with mixed motivations. The conclusion was that ***external motivations can weaken or displace internal motivations***. Giving children material rewards for doing their homework can, for example, have the effect—even if unintentional—of taking the place of interest in the subject, or stifling the desire to learn. Promising a ball to those who empty their pantry at home for the sake of those in need is more likely to elicit competition to obtain a prize—the ball—than it is to stir up a feeling of solidarity with the less fortunate. In other words, the most

---

[100] Wrzesniewski, A., Schwartz, B., Cong, X., Kane, M., Omar, A., & Kolditz, T. (2014). Multiple types of motives don't multiply the motivation of West Point cadets. *Proceedings of the National Academy of Sciences of the United States of America, 111*(30), 10.990–10.995.

fundamental and "imperfect" motivations could suppress or impede higher and more altruistic motivations.

"Educational" apps and websites

In the same way, we might ask ourselves about the effects of winning points on self-proclaimed educational games on certain apps or websites. They are called "educational" games, but are in fact more entertainment than anything.

Further, in a study entitled "Game-based Learning: Latest Evidence and Future Directions," the National Foundation for Education Research concluded, "Despite some promising results, the current literature does not evidence adequately the presumed link between motivation, attitudes to learning and learning outcomes."[101]

The problem with these supposedly "educational" websites is that the games are directed by a program. These algorithm-driven learning or gaming platforms incorporate persuasive design to keep kids online as long as possible. Furthermore, they are usually designed with a reward structure. These "games" motivate children, but do they have a positive effect on their learning? Given that studies are unable to establish that these games improve academic performance, it is possible that they stifle our children's internal and altruistic motivations in favour of external ones. There is cause for concern.

It is also important to examine claims that certain EdTech solutions not only increase engagement, but also improve students' cognitive abilities. As explained above, in the absence of studies supporting clear cognitive advantages of these technologies, *schools and teachers must understand that*

---

[101] Perrotta, C., Featherstone, G., Aston, H., & Houghton, E. (2013). Game-based learning: Latest evidence and future directions. *NFER Research Programme: Innovation in Education.* Slough, United Kingdom: National Foundation for Educational Research.

we are still at the experimental stage; they should consequently be cautious and foresighted when introducing these digital technologies into education. The industry as well as researchers involved in measuring the benefits of commercial products must be honest when they disclose their results, specifying that the "educational" character of these products has not advanced past the experimental phase.

For example, certain applications available on the market with the generic label of "brain training" offer an early stimulation of executive functions by means of digital platforms. There is no consensus in the literature on the positive effects of these applications. A review of such programs[102] indicated that:

1) there is a significant body of evidence that they improve performance in the specific tasks that were evaluated;

2) less evidence shows that these programs improve performance in related tasks; and

3) there is little evidence that they improve daily cognitive performance in general.

Besides the side effects that have led pediatric associations to recommend limiting the use of these technologies in early childhood (recommendations that are incidentally often ignored in the advertising and packaging of these products), the sort of benefits that these applications offer suggests an essentially behavioural approach (the improvement comes from

---

[102] Melby-Lervåg, M., & Hulme, C. (2013). Is working memory training effective? A meta-analytic review. *Developmental Psychology, 49*(2), 270–291; Simons, D.J., Boot, W.R., Charness, N., Gathercole, S.E., Chabris, C.F., Hambrick, D.Z., & Stine-Morrow, E.A.L. (2016). Do "brain-training" programs work? *Psychological Science in the Public Interest, 17*(3), 103–186.

mechanical repetition)—and one that is meaningless. These products work primarily on the basis of external motivations.

Learning to read and write from a screen

Many studies warn against replacing exercise books with screens. We all know that learning to read and write are essential for academic success and that the first step towards learning to read is recognizing letters, which will in turn determine if our children will be good readers or not.

In a study[103] that observed seven-year-old children learning to read, learning from active writing was compared to passively looking at the letters. The study, published in *Frontiers in Psychology*, revealed that **motor activity *(writing by hand)* was essential for learning to read**. These results confirmed a previous study that noted that the recognition of letters was more firmly established and more lasting in students who had written them by hand than in those who had typed them on a keyboard.[104] These results confirm the importance that certain pedagogues, notably Maria Montessori, placed on sensory experience in the process of learning to read and write. Another study[105] demonstrated that students who took notes on their laptop had worse results on more abstract conceptual questions than students who took notes by hand, even in the absence of distraction and controlling for the effect of multitasking.

---

[103] Kersey, A.J., & James, K.H. (2013). Brain activation patterns resulting from learning letter forms through active self-production and passive observation in young children. *Frontiers in Psychology, 4*, 567.

[104] Longcamp, M., Boucard, C., Gilhodes, J.C., Anton, J.L., Roth, M., Nazarian, B., & Velay, J.L. (2008). Learning through hand- or typewriting influences visual recognition of new graphics shapes: Behavioral and functional imaging evidence. *Journal of Cognitive Neuroscience, 20*(5), 802–815.

[105] Mueller, P.A. (2014). The pen is mightier than the keyboard: Advantages of longhand over laptop note taking. *Psychological Science, 25*(6).

Although a replication study challenged these conclusions,[106] another study published in 2019 confirmed them.[107] Since the question is not definitively resolved, further research on this subject will be necessary.

As far as reading comprehension is concerned, a study revealed that students who read print texts had better results on reading comprehension tests than students who read texts online.[108] In another study,[109] students were asked what their preferred format was for reading comprehension: print or digital. Students displayed a clear preference for digitized texts. However, their performance was inconsistent with these preferences. Although there was no difference between the two formats when it came to understanding the main idea of the text, comprehension was superior in the printed medium for the specific issues contained in it. A literature review[110] of studies from 1992 to 2017 indicated that students understand information in print better than digital information when the text is longer than one page. The authors suggested that this result can be attributed to the disruptive effect of needing to

[106] Morehead, K., Dunlosky, J., & Rawson, K.A. (2019). How much mightier is the pen than the keyboard for note-taking? A replication and extension of Mueller and Oppenheimer (2014). *Educational Psychology Review, 31*(3), 753–780.

[107] Arreola, H., Flores, A.N., Latham, A., MacNew, H., & Vu, K.P.L. (2019, July). Does the use of tablets lead to more information being recorded and better recall in short-term memory tasks? *International Conference on Human-Computer Interaction.* Springer, Cham, 292–302.

[108] Mangen, A., Walgermo, B.R., & Bronnick, K. (2013). Reading linear text on paper versus computer screen: Effects on reading comprehension. *International Journal of Educational Research, 58,* 61–68.

[109] Singer, L.M., & Alexander, P.A. (2017). Reading across mediums: Effects of reading digital and print texts on comprehension and calibration. *The Journal of Experimental Education, 85*(1), 155–172.

[110] Singer, L.M., & Alexander, P.A. (2017). Reading on paper and digitally: What the past decades of empirical research reveal. *Review of Educational Research, 87*(6), 1007–1041.

scroll down without being able to see the text as a whole in physical space.

In 2019, a research group composed of 200 university professors published its conclusions from an analysis of 54 studies on the subject:

> Research shows that paper remains the preferred reading medium for longer single texts, especially when reading for deeper comprehension and retention, and that paper best supports long-form reading of informational texts. Reading long-form texts is invaluable for a number of cognitive achievements, such as concentration, vocabulary building and memory.[111]

Thus, there is no doubt for the experts that EdTech cannot replace books, nor can it substitute for classrooms and teachers. But then, what do we do when we find ourselves in the midst of a pandemic?

---

[111] Evolution of Reading in the Age of Digitisation. (2019). Stavanger declaration concerning the future of reading. European Cooperation in Science and Technology. https://ereadcost.eu/wp-content/uploads/2019/01/StavangerDeclaration.pdf

Chapter 14
What to Do in a Pandemic

It is better to debate a question without settling it than to settle a question without debating it.
Joseph Joubert, South African politician

What about the online classes that many of our children participated in during the pandemic? As explained previously, in chapter 7, the AAP does not discourage communication via conference call (on FaceTime, Skype, or WhatsApp, for example) between children and people who are an important part of their everyday lives. This exception, which was initially intended for children separated from parents serving abroad in the armed forces, conceivably applies to live, online classes in circumstances like the pandemic we experienced. There should therefore be no cause for concern about secondary effects of such online classes. This does not mean, however, that they provide the best context for a child to learn in, especially for younger children, who mainly learn through interpersonal relationships and human interaction. Indeed, if we have been able to draw any lessons on this subject from the pandemic, it is the realization that having a teacher present in the same space as a child is a luxury that we should never dispense with without having serious reasons for doing so. Where in-class instruction is possible during the pandemic, priority should, as far as possible, be given to this model.

A statement[112] on this subject, signed by 100 experts and advocacy organizations, was published during the summer of

---

[112] Campaign for a Commercial-Free Childhood. (2020). A statement on EdTech and education policy during the pandemic.

2020 by the organization Campaign for a Commercial-Free Childhood. This statement reminds us that EdTech solutions are spearheaded by technology companies, for the purpose of acquiring an increasingly greater share of the global market in the education industry—currently worth $10 billion.[113] It warns against the temptation of systematically resorting to EdTech solutions during the pandemic, calling them simplistic and risky for children's health and privacy, and noting that they have not been proven to have academic benefits. The signatories underline the fundamental role of teachers and urge authorities and the education community to employ their creativity in order to find educational solutions that are rooted in reality.

Here are the recommendations outlined in this statement:

- **Limit screen time.** Use technology only when necessary for communication, collaboration, research, or facilitating creative expressions of student learning. Algorithm-driven adaptive learning platforms, gamified learning, and similar apps that incorporate persuasive design to keep kids online should be avoided.

- **Embrace teachers and relationships over EdTech.** Teachers engage learners better than EdTech, and learners engage better when learning is authentic. Remote learning, when needed, should be driven by human interactions and designed to maximize student engagement and agency through use of project- and place-based pedagogies and other self-directed projects.

https://commercialfreechildhood.org/edtech_statement/

[113] Lunden, I. (2019, February 28). ClassDojo, an app to help teachers and parents communicate better, raises $35M [Blog post]. Retrieved from https://social.techcrunch.com/2019/02/28/classdojo-an-app-to-help-teachers-and-parents-communicate-better-raises-35m

- **Maximize offline, hands-on learning.** Students, particularly younger children and children with special needs, learn better offline and hands-on. Therefore, schools have an obligation to maximize offline, hands-on learning – even if students are at home – by encouraging structured activities such as reading actual books, writing by hand, art, movement, outdoor play, real-world math projects, and nature exploration. During remote learning, schools must find ways to support families by providing physical books and supplies, in recognition of the fact that not all families are in a position to provide these things.

- **Avoid hasty purchases and decisions** during the pandemic that may lead to the overuse of EdTech for many years to follow. Instead, invest in educators.

- **Privacy matters.** Schools must understand and mitigate any privacy risks before assigning a platform or service to students. Schools should avoid services that do not clearly delineate who will have access to students' sensitive data and for what purpose. Schools should also not assign platforms or apps that contain advertising, including upselling students and their families on premium versions, thereby exacerbating inequalities among students.

According to technology company executives, EdTech solutions in schools are a preferred way for children to be the protagonists of their education, especially during a time of pandemic. What is the reasoning behind this claim? Certain voices in pedagogy argue that children can and should learn by themselves, without guidance. This is known as *pure discovery learning.* Thus, they say that educational technologies are a privileged means for children to "take the reins of their education." Certain voices also speak of the education system as being an obstacle to learning. For example, Roger Schank, an expert on artificial intelligence, goes even further when he proposes establishing a database that would allow students to learn completely "by themselves."

Is this possible for a child or a young student? What happens, for example, when children 2, 6, 10, or even 14 years old find themselves alone in a five-million-book library? Or when children, in the middle of a pandemic, spend 8 hours per day using algorithm-based apps and programs, and cannot find anyone to explain the material to them? What sort of knowledge do they acquire? What does this knowledge mean? Studies do not in fact support educational methods like "pure discovery learning" in children, as children cannot make connections with principles or pedagogical material and discovery will not in itself help them make sense of what they learn.[114] This is due to the fact that, as quoted earlier, "all teaching comes from pre-existing knowledge."[115]

Who then must organize the plan of studies so that learning is based on previous knowledge and will in turn serve as a foundation for what follows? The teacher, of course. *Learning does not spring up magically; children need an intermediary who can mediate between them and their environment, helping them to discover in an ordered manner.*

---

[114] Mayer, R.E. (2004). Should there be a three-strikes rule against pure discovery learning? *American Psychologist, 59*, 14–19; Kirschner, P.A., Sweller, J., & Clark, R.E. (2006). Why minimal guidance during instruction does not work: An analysis of the failure of constructivist, discovery, problem-based, experiential, and inquiry-based teaching. *Journal of Educational Psychology, 41*, 75–86.

[115] Aquinas, T. (1953). *Questiones disputatae de veritate* (J. V. McGlynn, Trans.). Chicago, IL: Henry Regnery Company. (Original work published c. 1259).

Whether we are in the midst of a pandemic or not, the nature of children always remains the same. Consequently, *in order for the Internet to be a good learning tool, or in order to take advantage of a five-million-book library, students must first have acquired the basic knowledge that will allow them to understand what they are researching, how to find this information, and why they should look for it.* They must have developed a sense of relevancy and self-control to motivate them to carry out their research and filter out irrelevant information that they might encounter along the way. Under these conditions, the Internet can be an excellent learning tool. However, it is unlikely that they will be able to develop and solidify a sense of relevancy or the capacity for self-control in front of a screen. As we explained earlier, before diving into the world of the Internet, children must have developed a series of qualities that will allow them to manage their behaviour positively: social competencies, a sense of privacy that will allow them to distinguish between public space and private space, good judgment, self-control, the strength of will to filter out external stimuli, etc. *A sense of relevancy, for example, is defined by a series of criteria (I shouldn't share secrets with strangers, I should compare and contrast information before believing it, etc.) which children develop at a young age, in the offline world; in the real world, far from screens; in their interpersonal relationships, by means of an education that will allow them to make sense of what they learn.*

Certain defenders of EdTech solutions confuse the external motivation that screens elicit in children and the fact that students must "take the reins of their education." They plead the cause of technology use so that children might be the protagonists of their education. This rationale, although interesting at first sight, is mistaken. Why? Let us analyze this argument closely.

We can all agree that children and teenagers should in part take the reins of their education. But the novelty effect and the accelerated pace of technology, or the *external motivation* factor (like so-called called "educational" games) do not necessarily lead children to take the reins of their education—quite the contrary. ***In fact, it is not the student sitting in front of the screen that holds the reins, it is the "smart," algorithm-driven application on the device. Students, as well as teachers, are both relegated to a back-seat role.*** The individualized education offered by these technologies has nothing to do with a genuinely personal attention, which only a person can offer, whether there is a pandemic or not.

Perhaps, without realizing it, we are confusing two different ideas. Growing up *in front* of a screen and growing up *behind* one are not the same thing. But what does this all mean?

Chapter 15
In Front of or *Behind* the Screen?

All who thoughtlessly make use of the achievements of science and
technology without wanting to understand more about them than a
cow does about the botany of the plants on which it blissfully
grazes, ought to be ashamed of themselves.
Albert Einstein

Most people make the mistake of thinking design is what it looks
like. That's not what we think design is. It's not just what it looks
like and feels like. Design is how it works.
Steve Jobs

The majority of parents want to offer their children all the opportunities they can to become—to the extent that they are able—innovative and creative. Some parents, with the best intentions in the world, purchase a tablet for their four-year-old child and a desktop computer or state-of-the-art smartphone for their eight-year-old, thinking that this will increase their chances of success. When all is said and done, their bedroom ends up having more screens than windows.

Steve Jobs spent a large part of his childhood in his garage at home, where he learned from his adoptive father, who was a mechanic and a carpenter, to work with his hands and to assemble and disassemble television sets and radios. He did not spend hours in front of screens, passively consuming material. He worked *behind* them. During this period of his life, he shared his passion for building electronic devices with his neighbours, Bill Fernandez and Steve Wozniak, who also played a pivotal role in the development of the first Mac computer.

Now we are doubtlessly better able to understand a 2014 *New York Times* article that reported that **Steve Jobs was** *hesitant to allow his children to use electronic devices.*[116] In fact, Steve Jobs did not allow his children to use the iPad and limited their use of other technologies. In this article, the journalist delivers the conclusions of various interviews he conducted with executives of technology companies. One of the founders of Blogger and Twitter, for example, stated that his children use physical books rather than tablets. Among those interviewed, there were many who did not allow their children to use a laptop before the age of 14 and the Internet before the age of 17, and they unanimously refused to allow these technologies into their children's bedrooms. Do they know something that we do not? The secret is very simple: *the best preparation for becoming technologically creative, innovative, and entrepreneurial does not consist in spending hours and hours in front of a screen, but rather in freely experimenting.* In 1996, Jobs said in an interview granted to the magazine *Wired*[117] that "People are thinking less than they used to. It's primarily because of television." Being innovative cannot be attributed to knowing how to use the latest iPhone or iPad model; we have seen that these devices are designed so that anyone can easily use them. Thus, for Steve Jobs, innovation meant "saying no to 1,000 things." He did not want his children to be captivated by a deafening screen. He did not want them to be transformed into "suckers for irrelevancy," wasting their time with technologies that are programmed to become obsolete. He preferred that they prepare to become innovators. And in order to accomplish this in the world of digital media, it is essential to spend time *behind* the screen and

---

[116] Bilton, N. (2014, September 10). Steve Jobs was a low-tech parent. *The New York Times*. https://www.nytimes.com/2014/09/11/fashion/steve-jobs-apple-was-a-low-tech-parent.html

[117] Wolf, G. (1996, February 4). Steve Jobs: The next insanely great thing. *Wired*. https://www.wired.com/1996/02/jobs-2/

not *in front* of it. Einstein said, "The wellspring of all technical achievements is the divine curiosity and playful instinct of the tinkering and thoughtful researcher, and, no less, the constructive imagination of the technical inventor." Once more, it is crucial that we do not confuse *play* and *entertainment.*

Even when working behind the screen (rather than in front of it), one must have more than simple technical know-how. How does one distinguish a good programmer from one that fails to stand out from the crowd? Simple technical competencies are not enough. Danny Thorpe, a well-known programmer who has worked for Microsoft and Google, states, "Programming without an overall architecture or design in mind is like exploring a cave with only a flashlight: You don't know where you've been, you don't know where you're going, and you don't know quite where you are." It is essential to understand the context. Indeed, in order to devote oneself to computer programming and be successful at it, one needs far more than simple technical competence. Woodie Flowers, a professor of mechanical engineering at the Massachusetts Institute of Technology, says much the same: "I believe that education and training are different. To me, training is an essential commodity that will certainly be outsourced to digital systems and be dramatically improved in the process. Education is much more subtle and complex and is likely to be accomplished through mentorship or apprentice-like interactions between a learner and an expert."[118] And he adds, "Education is the source of comparative advantage for students."

Flowers speaks of an education "accomplished through [...] interactions between a learner and an expert," and thus, of a personalized and human education. That is the education that

[118] Flowers, W. (2012). Teach talk: A contrarian view of MITx: What are we doing!? *MIT Faculty Newsletter, 24*(3).

is the source of comparative advantage for our children, not the individualized "education" offered by a tablet or notebook computer.

Is education necessarily incompatible with technology? Not at all. *There are in fact some technologies that, in the hands of children, do stir up a more active than passive attitude, such as programming, website design, or photography.* By way of example, at the age of 9, Carlos Pérez Naval became the youngest winner of the Young Wildlife Photographer of the Year contest, awarded for 50 years by the BBC in partnership with the Natural History Museum in London. His photographs witness to an exceptional sensitivity and appreciation for beauty.[119] Carlos began photographing flowers with a compact camera. Besides his talent, several determining factors made it possible for him to become one of the best photographers in his category. Among these are the fact that his parents are themselves photographers and were able to give him advice at any given time. In addition, his love for nature and his enthusiasm for the reality that he photographs are passions that he shares with his parents and that led him to spend a great deal of time with them. He said, "It isn't just for fun. My mom and dad also take photos and I go with them. We spend a lot of time together."[120]

We can now see how essential interpersonal relationships are for learning, and how fundamental they are for a human education that makes learning meaningful.

---

[119] See https://carlospereznaval.wordpress.com

[120] Valdés, I. (2014, October 29). Diez años, un escorpión y el Wildlife. *El País*.https://elpais.com/cultura/2014/10/27/actualidad/1414427149_703 842.html

Chapter 16
Personalized Education—Without the Person

Every child is unique. For this reason, education should be personalized. A personalized education is not the same thing as the individualized education offered by apps or websites. A personalized education is based on the idea that every person is an active being, capable of knowing and changing the world that surrounds him or her. The concept of an individualized education, on the other hand, relies on the fact that every individual is an organism that passively reacts to external stimuli, or to algorithm-driven applications, which are designed or programmed in such a way as to procure concrete results for each individual. The personalized-education approach relies on a conception of the person that recognizes the existence of internal and altruistic motivations, whereas the individualized-education approach relies primarily on external motivations.

But what is it that makes us unique? What contributes to the development and flourishing of our personal identity as well as our awareness of this identity? Daniel Siegel, a professor of biology and psychiatry at the University of California, Los Angeles, asserts that explicit memory (i.e., the capacity to consciously recall facts and events) is necessary for the development of a child's sense of identity, and that this explicit memory is based on interpersonal relationships. This is how human beings begin to be aware that they "are" in time and space.

> Recalling the order in which events in the world occur allows the child to develop a sense of time and sequence. [...This makes it possible] to identify context and to create a four-dimensional sense of the self in the world across time.[121]

This autobiographical memory is the result of interpersonal experiences; the memory of what one has done, said, and heard; and the internal reflections made in light of this experience—all of which contributes to developing a sense of personal identity. All of this answers the question, "Who am I?" According to Siegel, interpersonal experiences have a direct effect on the development of explicit memory. Thus, our own actions have an effect on the people around us, and the opposite is also true: the actions of others affect us and help to shape our personality.

We learn in contact with reality. This is even more true for children, who need sensory and concrete, interpersonal experiences in order to understand the world and themselves. This can be seen in the fact that very young children do not yet possess a solid semantic memory (memory of conceptual knowledge). From the age of 2, their memory is instead autobiographical (memory of events lived through perceived experiences). This is the reason why children learn essentially through interpersonal relationships and their senses, not by means of abstract lectures or interactive screens—they need real experiences. This could also explain the *video deficit effect* that we mentioned in chapter 7: *young children learn better from an in-person demonstration than a virtual one.* For

---

121 Siegel, D. J. (2012). *The developing mind: How relationships and the brain interact to shape who we are.* New York, NY: The Guilford Press, p. 506.

the same reason, if we tell young children to stop crying but we raise our voices while doing so, or if we reprimand them for not respecting other people's things and punish them by confiscating their own, we risk encouraging the opposite of the desired behaviour.

It is well known that children do not remember their earliest experiences. We do not remember the first two years of our lives, in fact—a phenomenon known as *childhood amnesia*. Does this mean that experiences that happened before the age of 2 are unimportant? On the contrary. These experiences leave a trace in the brain, thereby forming an internal model, a point of reference, from which children understand the world and themselves. From the age of 2, these experiences begin to be retained by the autobiographical memory and hence shape our sense of personal identity. Consequently, everything that children experience through their five senses is more important than long, abstract explanations that they are given during this period (even if children do not remember events that occurred before the age of 2).

We can see, then, to what extent contact with reality and relationships with others at school, in class, at home, or with family, leave an impression and reinforce our sense of identity. Our personal (and also familial and cultural) autobiographical memory develops from interpersonal experiences of harmony, empathy, and compassion, experienced with the people around us. Thanks to these positive interpersonal experiences that reinforce our awareness of our unique identity (whether personal, familial, or cultural), we plant the roots of resilience that will later allow us to withstand the winds and tempests of life.

It is therefore indispensable that parents and teachers understand the true meaning of their role in education. Depending on the children or teenagers' stage of life, this role will mean catching their gaze and interpreting it, telling them true or fictional stories, helping them gauge the significance of their affective problems, tenderly correcting a fault, helping them to decipher their emotions, remembering a moving moment with them, showing them by our expression that a certain behaviour is unacceptable, being attentive to their needs, helping them to identify their strengths and weaknesses, etc. *Ultimately, it is a question of a series of profoundly human actions that digital devices cannot offer.*

What happens to children who have fewer opportunities for interpersonal experiences, because the mediator between them and reality is a screen? Siegel tells us that when children suffer from a lack of interpersonal experiences, they do not have sufficient contextual resources for understanding and orienting themselves. The implicit memory (the emotional memory, which does not require conscious thought) then takes over and fills in the gaps. If children or young teenagers have not had enough interpersonal experiences to allow them, by means of their memories, to become aware of their own identity, they will end up adopting the behaviour of the protagonist of their favourite Netflix show, the actions of a character in their favourite violent video games or of the people in the pornographic videos they watch secretly, or the tone of the text messages that fill the screen that they lug around in their pocket. When faced with aggression, children with an explicit memory deficient in positive interpersonal experiences can only have recourse to their implicit memory, to the violent reaction displayed by a character in Fortnite, a game that occupies the greater part of their weekends. When faced with frustrations, they will reproduce this reaction in order to fill the gap in their autobiographical memory. According to the

Academy of Child and Adolescent Psychiatry,[122] studies show that children tend to imitate what they see and hear in the media, which can result in a contagion effect among them. Children learn by imitation. This is a mechanism that has been well known since Montessori and Piaget.

When children have not yet consolidated their personal identity and do not have enough real models in their environment with which they can identify, they might have recourse to the digital environment to fill in the gaps, because the window of their virtual world becomes their primary vantage point. Ultimately, the virtual model to which they have been exposed, and their own feelings, perception of self, and personal identity merge into one. What is said and disseminated on Netflix, in video games, on pornography sites, and on social media pages, becomes *the* reference, *the* measure, *the* truth. These children then desire whatever they see in these windows and will look to satisfy their emotional needs by behaving according to what they see there, in the hopes of winning the approval of their peers. These children or teenagers imitate and desire to be imitated. This is what their sense of identity is reduced to. This path will distance them ever further from building up a genuinely personal and authentic sense of identity.

A European study[123] carried out on teenagers between the ages of 14 and 17 reported that adolescents this age need to feel affirmed. Rather than seeking this affirmation offline (in the real world), they look for it online, where, on the lookout for what their peers think of them, they seek to feel accepted and capable.

---

[122] Academy of Child and Adolescent Psychiatry. (2013). Children and the news. *Facts for Families, 67.*

[123] EU.NET.ADB. (2013). Investigación sobre conductas adictivas a Internet entre adolescentes europeos. EU NET ADB Consortium. http://www.injuve.es/sites/default/files/2013/03/publicaciones/FinalRe searchInternet-ES.pdf

According to this study, "affirmation can fill a void when it comes to adolescents with a deficit in offline social skills […]." The study concludes, "Adolescents with poor offline-skills development can feel strongly enabled and affirmed on the Internet, and are consequently more vulnerable to the development of 'dysfunctional Internet behaviour'" (notably, dependencies or the risk of developing them). The study also underlines that ***gambling, social media use, and computer gaming are factors that double the risk among adolescents of adopting dysfunctional behaviours***. Despite some of them supposedly having educational value, these activities can result in dependencies due to the reward factor (external motivation) associated with them.

Social skills acquired in the real world are the key to using digital media well, which reinforces the idea that ***the best preparation for the online world is the offline world***. It is important, for example, to have a sense of self-esteem that leads us to say, like Plutarch, "I don't need a friend who changes when I change and who nods when I nod; my shadow does that much better."

A sense of discretion and of privacy are good indicators that a person has consolidated his or her sense of self. Those who have a strong sense of self have a rich inner world that is their own and do not frivolously let just anyone into it. Children who are exposed to social media can have difficulty understanding all of these concepts. A mother told me about a troubling experience she had with this:

> *I had just given birth and my son was placed in an incubator because there had been complications with the delivery. This was very difficult because I was not able to hold him in my arms in the hours that followed his birth. After a while, my seventeen-year-old daughter showed up with her smartphone. She showed me a photo of my son in the incubator. She had posted it on Facebook and all her friends had seen him before I, his*

own mother, could hold him in my arms. I explained to my daughter that what she had done was very troubling to me. I discussed the importance of privacy and discretion with her. She didn't understand what the problem was. Even after my explanations, she could not understand how I felt.

Mark Zuckerberg, the founder of Facebook, has said that privacy is no longer a "social norm," as if a value such as privacy could ever become obsolete. Whatever the case may be, it is apparent that children who have grown up on social media will have difficulty developing a sense of discretion and privacy.

In order to have a richer autobiographical memory, life must be lived in person; it must be experienced directly, not through the lens of a smartphone. Clearly, digital technology can help us do this by reawakening memories of lived experiences, by means of photography or video recordings, for example. It can also help us to connect with those whom we cannot see in person because of distance, or self-isolation during a pandemic. It can also keep alive or revive a friendship that was formed independently of the Internet, thanks to useful tools like Skype or FaceTime. ***But we must explain to our children that a Wi-Fi connection is not the same thing as a human connection.*** One does not necessarily lead to the other. In fact, a 2019 study conducted by YouGov[124] in the United States indicates that millennials—the generation that uses social media the most—are the loneliest generation. About 30% of them say they do not have a best friend, 27% acknowledge that they do not have close friends, and 20% admit to not having any friends at all. Our children must be taught that connecting to Wi-Fi is not the same as meeting another person's gaze…. Is this why children are less and less able to

[124] Ballard, J. (2019, July 30). Millennials are the loneliest generation. *YouGov.* https://today.yougov.com/topics/lifestyle/articles-reports/2019/07/30/loneliness-friendship-new-friends-poll-survey

look someone in the eyes, or even just at the face? When we do not look at someone's face, it becomes difficult to interpret emotions, to pick up on the meaning of someone's facial expression. And, as the Arabic proverb goes, "He who doesn't understand a gaze will not understand a long explanation."

Confusing *personal* and *individual* attention results in the devaluation of interpersonal relationships. In public restrooms, the stalls afford an individualized moment (one of isolation, for greater privacy), but we cannot speak here of personal attention. This would be the case if there were people in the public restrooms available to help seniors who had, for example, mobility problems. Personal attention means the attention of one person to the needs of another. Hence, "one-to-one" programs (one device per student) do not guarantee a personalized education, but rather an individualized one, driven by algorithms, which is not the same thing. And **when children sit in front of a screen for 8 hours, there is an obvious loss of opportunities for interpersonal relationships, because there are a limited number of hours in a day**. Media use has a *displacement effect*, because it pilfers time from real experiences and opportunities for interpersonal relationships.

Personalized education is far more than a method, or a marketing pitch used in education. It is the consequence of a teacher realizing that students are each unique in their ability to understand the world around them in light of their search for meaning. Education must consequently be adapted to children's real needs and must take their innate desire to know and act into consideration. It is important that children be given *what their true nature demands* (e.g., sensory or interpersonal experiences), which is not always the same as *what they ask for* (e.g., technological stimuli, thrilling sensations). This is the delicate work that falls to parents and educators: distinguishing one thing from another. **Distinguishing between what children**

124

ask for and what their true nature demands is a task that requires the intervention of a sensitive parent or teacher; it cannot be accomplished by a digital tool (for which our children are no more than peripherals that react when connected to a device). Whatever investments are made in Silicon Valley, their devices and their applications' algorithms will never be capable of discernment, because discernment requires sensitivity. And sensitivity is profoundly human, not digital.

Studies show that secure attachment—the relationship of trust that results from a rich interpersonal relationship between a child and his or her parent—is stronger among children with coherent autobiographical memories whose past has been nourished by rich opportunities for interpersonal relationships. These relationships are able to give meaning to their present and to their future, thanks to the firm sense of self that results from them.[125] It is not only psychologists who are aware of this. Corporations are also interested in this mechanism, which they use to promote a stronger attachment to their brands, knowing that the best way to form this bond of trust is through storytelling. This is why experiential marketing—the idea of selling customers a product for the experience it provides them during marketing or consumption—is so popular. In 1998, Pine and Gilmore, the authors of *The Experience Economy*,[126] explained that when someone is paid for a physical product, they are in the goods market; if they are paid for the activities they offer, they are in the service market; and if it is for time spent with them, they are in the experience market. *The virtual world is permeated through and through by experiential*

---

[125] Siegel, D.J. (2012). *The developing mind: How relationships and the brain interact to shape who we are.* New York, NY: The Guilford Press, p. 506.

[126] Pine, B.J., & Gilmore, J.H. (1999). *The experience economy.* Boston, MA: Harvard Business School Press.

marketing, which works on the basis of our emotions, making use of the fact that young people are eager for new sensations that fascinate. We know that the media to which young people devote the most time are videos.[127] Consumption skyrocketed between 2015 and 2019: 56% of youth between the ages of 8 and 12 (compared to 24% in 2015) and 69% of those between the ages of 9 and 18 (compared to 34% in 2015) say that they watch them every day. Advertising designers compete for young people's attention with storylines and imagery that are increasingly faster-paced and more shocking. However, what is missing in these marketing campaigns is that these stories do not come to us in the context of an interpersonal relationship, a lived experience. Consequently, they might affect us emotionally, but generally speaking, they do not help to build up our autobiographical memory. Instead, they merely fill in the gaps, especially for children or teenagers who have had few opportunities for personal relationships, as we explained earlier. It is just as absurd to be moved by these marketing campaigns as it is when we receive birthday wishes from Amazon, Christmas greetings from Coca-Cola, or congratulations from Toys "R" Us for the birth of a child. Generally speaking, these efforts leave us indifferent. No sane person is moved by this sort of publicity; we understand perfectly the difference between this sort of message and a card sent by a friend.

> *"Did you buy your daughter a smartphone this year?"*

> *"Of course! I don't want my eleven-year-old daughter to be socially isolated. I want her to have friends like everyone else."*

---

[127] Common Sense Media. (2017). Fact sheet. The Common Sense census: Media use by kids age zero to eight. https://www.commonsensemedia.org/research/the-common-sense-census-media-use-by-kids-age-zero-to-eight-2017; Rideout, V., & Robb, M.B. (2019). The Common Sense census: Media use by tweens and teens. San Francisco, CA: Common Sense Media.

Our children must live life in person. They must learn what a genuine friendship is, that it is more than exchanging emojis and "likes," or conversations on Instagram and Snapchat, often filled with abbreviations and acronyms. *Friendship means taking the time to meet up in person, being available, speaking gently, understanding one another, listening to each other's tone of voice, looking at the other's facial expression, interpreting his or her gaze.* It is spending time together without constantly checking the time and without letting the other interrupt to respond to unknown people in 2D. It is arranging to meet without a specific goal, without wanting anything in exchange. It is standing together silently while looking out at a magnificent view. It is going for a coffee and talking about Christmas, the latest rainfall, or things that are not necessarily useful, but are not any less important. Yet now this is something rare; we do not have time for real life, because we spend almost all of our "free" moments in front of a screen. Being asked "How's it going?"—sincerely, in order to *really* know how it is going, without being afraid of a boring response, without character or time limits—is something priceless. A true friend does not want to know your schedule or the number of texts you have to respond to; does not want to know if you are busy or *really* busy. A true friend does not want you to tell them that you made a sacrifice to see them because you are *so* busy. They will never make you feel that way. It is not because a true friend does not care whether you are busy or not—it is because they want to know more, because you are truly important to them. A friend is available and gives you their full, undivided attention, that attention which is the measuring stick of love and a pure form of generosity. *This is the real friendship for which our children must make space in their stressed-out-CEO schedules and their frenetic digital lives on social media. Is it not therefore ironic that we buy them all these*

devices in order to break down the walls of social isolation? We are human and we need human experiences; we need to feel empathy for others and we need others to feel empathy for us. And if the pandemic has made one thing apparent, it is the incalculable value of physicality, of being present in person. Before the pandemic, digital technology was synonymous with status and progress, whereas with the widespread isolation mandated during the pandemic, it is human interaction that has become a luxury...

Chapter 17
Lost Empathy

I love mankind... it's people I can't stand!
Charles M. Schulz, *Peanuts*

A study[128] at the University of Michigan that looked at 14,000 students from 1979 to 2009 concluded that the youth of 2009 were 40% less empathetic than those of 20 or 30 years earlier, noting that the decline began in the year 2000. The researchers attributed this decrease in empathy to the appearance of social media.

To illustrate this phenomenon, we need only think of the 2011 Grammy Awards gala, when a journalist suffered what seemed to be stroke, struggling to speak during her news report. In the seconds that followed, the video went viral on YouTube and social media, garnering thousands of likes and insensitive comments encouraging people to watch and share the video, which was later labelled one of the five most memorable moments of the Grammy Awards night on AOL.com.[129]

Screens can present a barrier between reality and ourselves. What is more is that they can trivialize reality, because the manner in which we perceive reality in the

---

[128] Konrath, S.H., O'Brien, E.H., & Hsing, C. (2011). Changes in dispositional empathy in American college students over time: A meta-analysis. *Personality and Social Psychology Review, 15*(2), 180–198.

[129] Small, G., & Vorgan, G. (2011, February 18). Is the internet killing empathy? *CNN.* https://www.cnn.com/2011/OPINION/02/18/small.vorgan.internet.empathy/index.html

imaginary world (whether online or in a book) tends to be different from the way we do it in the real world. Thus, Simone Weil said:

> Imaginary evil is romantic and varied; real evil is gloomy, monotonous, barren, boring. Imaginary good is boring; real good is always new, marvelous, intoxicating. Therefore, 'imaginative literature' is either boring or immoral (or a mixture of both). It only escapes from this alternative if in some way it passes over to the side of reality through the power of art—and only genius can do that.

This "genius" develops in people who have the sensitivity necessary to grasp reality and enough talent to reflect the beauty and splendour of the real world by means of the imaginary. When we enjoy classic films or books, we realize that these are in fact the works of those "geniuses," which have been able to withstand the passage of time.

Sensitivity is the prerequisite for empathy. In terms of interpersonal relationships, it is through sensitivity that we are able to establish authentic relationships, that we genuinely connect and enter into harmony with the people around us. *Sensitivity allows us to wonder at what surrounds us, to take nothing for granted. It allows us to "feel" everything, to live life intensely, not as a spectator, but in the first person, to more easily put ourselves in another's shoes, which is the very essence of empathy.*

We all have a concrete sensitivity that allows us to be attuned to others, to understand them, without necessarily agreeing with them. The etymological meaning of the word *compassion* is "to suffer with," hence, those who have not experienced suffering have difficulty feeling compassion for someone else. Simone Weil said that "Human beings are so made that the ones who do the crushing feel nothing; it is the person crushed who feels what is happening. Unless one has placed oneself on the side of the oppressed, to feel with them, one cannot understand."[130] And, speaking of compassion, she adds, "The capacity to give one's attention to a sufferer is a very rare and difficult thing; it is almost a miracle. It *is* a miracle. Nearly all those who think they have this capacity do not possess it."[131] It is difficult to have empathy in the virtual world, a world where there are no faces, only distant profile pictures. Others are different than us, they are not simply the creation of our imagination. In the virtual world, "others" *are* often the creation of our imagination, because the information that we have on them is limited to the 160 characters of their online profile. It is not possible to love what one does not know.

Sensitivity leads to empathy, and empathy makes us more sensitive and human. It is a virtuous cycle that nourishes certain qualities that are indispensable for the process of seeking the perfection that is possible to us. Why? Kant said that "Education is the development in the individual of all the perfection of which he is capable." Sensitivity makes it possible to distinguish between what is essential and what is not. Insensitive people often place their trust in appearances, at the surface level. They give importance to the form as an end in itself, rather than as a reflection of its essence. For example, they consider it essential for their children to speak multiple languages in order to be able to communicate with people from around the world, but do not attach importance to learning empathy, which is a necessary quality for truly understanding others, not only those who are distant from us, but also those who are right next to us. Sensitive people go further; they see what the eye cannot. For example, a sensitive parent in search

---

[130] Weil, S. (1978). *Lectures on philosophy.* (H. Price, Trans.). Press Syndicate of the University of Cambridge. (Original work published 1959), p. 139.
[131] Weil, S. (2009). *Waiting on God.* Routledge. (Original work published 1942), p. 36.

of a daycare or preschool will place more importance on the adult-child ratio, group size, and his or her personal criteria—after seeing the place first-hand—than to rankings, or the importance given to the use of technology according to the criteria in vogue. A sensitive teacher understands that children bursting with energy on a rainy afternoon do not need a fast-paced movie, but a story. Sensitivity is what allows us to better understand our true nature, to know what it is capable of or not and to discern what is or is not appropriate for it. Sensitive people who devote themselves to education are educators *par excellence*. On the other hand, an educator who lacks sensitivity will not be an educator, even if he or she is devoted full-time to education with the best of intentions. In education, "good intentions" are never an argument in themselves, and still less when it comes to justifying what does not make sense.

Violence, increasingly accessible on our children's portable screens, has an obvious effect on their degree of empathy. Some say that children are perfectly able to distinguish between fiction and reality and that violent material does not affect them. People who do not control the content that their children watch very often say things like, "It's nothing to worry about," "You shouldn't exaggerate," "It's a question of balance," or "It's just a matter of sensibility." These assertions are good illustrations of the poor understanding of the very essence of childhood and the repercussions that watching violent or inhuman scenes has on young children's behaviour and their way of seeing the world. It is difficult to imagine that a parent or teacher with a modicum of sense could arrive at the conclusion that spending hours killing and punching in a video game has no effect on a child. ***Asserting that what young children watch "doesn't necessarily affect them" is an insult to common sense.***

The American Academy of Child and Adolescent Psychiatry summarizes the results of many studies conducted on the effects of violent television content,[132] which indicate that children who view this sort of content:

- Become desensitized to the horror of violence;

- Become increasingly accepting of violence as a means to resolve problems;

- Imitate the violence they observe;

- Identify themselves with characters in the violent material, whether the victims or the aggressors.

It concluded that the number of hours spent watching television, even apart from the issue of violent content, should be moderated, because it takes away from the time that they could be devoting to other activities that are important for their healthy development, like reading, playing with friends, developing motor skills, or discovering other healthy leisure activities.

Violence anesthetizes our children's sensitivity. When they are continually exposed to it on screen, they cease to feel what is human, what is true. It inhibits them from feeling empathy or compassion. When children lose their sensitivity due to violence or overstimulation, or because this sensitivity is seen as a weakness, they become "Teflon" children. Teflon is an antiadhesive non-stick material. Thus, nothing affects these children; nothing stirs up wonder in them; nothing truly matters to them. With such children, education becomes impossible, as much for their parents as for their teachers. Now, *to educate is not to desensitize children in order to prepare them to live in a cruel world without it*

---

[132] Academy of Child and Adolescent Psychiatry. (2011). Children and TV violence. *Facts for Families, 13.*

causing them suffering; it is, on the contrary, to make them more compassionate so that they can make the world more human.

Children who have grown up with on-screen violence, with few opportunities for interpersonal relationships, will have difficulty describing their emotions, engaging in introspection, taking responsibility for their actions, or knowing themselves. And as for their relationships with others, they will struggle to make eye contact, interpret facial expressions, anticipate human reactions, or put themselves in another's shoes.

When children lose their sensitivity, they find themselves on the lookout for strong emotions, which they seek through screens: violent video games or movies, pornography, or an abusive use of social media. The result is that *we live in a society crammed full of virtual emotions; we seek emotional thrills, but we have lost the ability to grasp reality through the senses.*

Chapter 18
The Thought Deficit

We who have assimilated the smartphone and are constantly connected to the Internet, we who have been transformed into "iPeople," we are far more powerful than the rest of Homo sapiens, *because we are better able to adapt to the new cultural landscape. We are practically omniscient.*

Pere Marqués, consultant for the introduction of tablets to classrooms

Accumulating information allows, at the very most, the development of theories and the resolution of technical problems. "Thinking," on the other hand, requires courage. W. B. Yeats said that "It takes more courage to dig deep in the dark corners of your own soul and the back alleys of your society than it does for a soldier to fight on a battle field." Thought makes it possible to have an internal dialogue, to take a critical look at our own actions and the extent to which they affect others. This dialogue with oneself requires interior silence, empathy, and sensitivity, in order to put oneself in another's place and understand the intentions of the people and world around us.

However, the habit of thinking seems to be increasingly rare. A study published in the journal *Science*[133] shows that 25% of women and 67% of men who participated preferred to self-administer a small electric shock rather than remain sitting in an empty room for 6 to 15 minutes, with nothing else to distract themselves than their own thoughts. The Indian philosopher Debendranath Tagore seems therefore to have

---

[133] Wilson, T.D., Reinhard, D.A., Westgate, E.C., Gilbert, D.T., Ellerberck, N., Hahn, C., Brown, C.L., & Shaked, A. (2014). Just think: The challenges of the disengaged mind. *Science, 345*(6.192), 75–77.

been right to declare that "Man goes into the noisy crowd to drown his own clamour of silence." Nowadays, people often turn to web browsing to escape from being alone with their own thoughts, which is frankly better than an electric shock.

The neuromyth of the unlimited cognitive potential of our children, easy access to any sort of information through the digital world, and the mistaken belief that our children potentially have the mind of a genius has led us to what we could define as an obsession with accumulating or finding information, without necessarily understanding its context. *The technological multitasking that transforms our children into "suckers for irrelevancy" paralyses deep reflection. The online generation has access to all sorts of information, but lacks context. It is fascinated, but does not wonder; it incessantly desires what calls out to its instincts, but has no deep aspirations; it allows itself to be easily ensnared by the superficial.* "A 33-year-old slice of cake from Prince Charles and Princess Diana's 1981 wedding has sold at auction for $1,375";[134] "Brazil woman falls in manhole after car hits her scooter."[135] Does it make *sense* to interrupt my homework, my work, a personal conversation, or even my free time, or to shorten my sleep at night to read this piece of news? Is there nothing else to do that is more interesting or constructive?

University professors see every day with their own eyes the lack of critical thinking, ability to synthesize information, and

---

[134] CTV News. (2014, August 29). Royal slice: Piece of Princess Diana's wedding cake sells for $1,375. https://www.ctvnews.ca/world/royal-slice-piece-of-princess-diana-s-wedding-cake-sells-for-1-375-1.1983819

[135] News Colony. (2020, August 7). Brazil woman falls in manhole after car hits her scooter. https://newscolony.com/brazil-woman-falls-in-manhole-after-car-hits-her-scooter

originality in the work that they receive, not to mention the considerable increase in spelling mistakes.

After hearing about the marvels of EdTech in a school meeting, and learning about the beginnings of the digital revolution in the school, a parent speaks to the principal.

Parent: "What about spelling? Are you going to teach it to kids?"
Principal: "Don't worry, there are spell checkers for that."

The Internet has become a mental hard drive for many students, who, instead of thinking, simply turn to copying and pasting. A chimpanzee connected to the Internet is still a chimpanzee. What sort of professionals are we preparing for the world of tomorrow? What happens with these young people who have supposedly evolved into "iPeople"? Thomas Moore said that "To be educated, a person doesn't have to know much or be informed, but he or she does have to have been exposed vulnerably to the transformative events of an engaged human life." And he added, "One of the greatest problems of our time is that many are schooled but few are educated."

External motivation, a consequence of using digital media passively, helps to convert young people into conformists who do not want to stand out. For a conformist, thinking is dangerous, because it can lead to one standing out from the pack. A conformist hates attracting attention.

Thinking is grasping all the nuances of reality in order to adjust oneself to them; it is being capable of critical reflection, of introspection, empathy, creativity, and a search for meaning. All of this must be part of an education in which children are the protagonists, not simply passive observers.

Simply filling oneself with data and information can be likened to filling a white sheet of paper with black dots. When the paper is filled with dots, everything becomes dark and confused. There is no longer any meaning. But human thought makes it possible to connect and organize the dots in order to create a meaningful drawing. Steve Jobs said that creativity is no more than connecting the dots, and, referring to creative people's ability to connect experiences and synthesize things, "the reason they were able to do that was that they've had more experiences or they have thought more about their experiences than other people. […] The broader one's understanding of the human experience, the better design we will have." Once again, we can see the importance of context, of authentically human experiences, and of personal attention in education. An excess of time spent in front of a screen is time taken from these experiences. And the time invested in very "content-rich" interpersonal relationships is the best preparation for making prudent use of digital media. We are not speaking of passively lived experiences filtered through a screen, but rather those which we experience in the first person. As Aldous Huxley said, "Experience is not what happens to you; it's what you do with what happens to you."

When we attach more importance to accumulating or having access to information than to deep reflection, we get children who are ever more technically prepared, but less and less able to adapt themselves to reality and find meaning in what they do. This overdose of information does not leave room for the dialogue that everyone should have with him- or herself. These children will later fall prey to fake news, because they are not prepared to understand the context of the information. They will later be fertile ground for ideological manipulation, unable to judge or think about the consequences of their actions, because they will not have devoted enough of their time to thinking.

An authentic education necessarily involves a search for meaning. For this purpose, students need to understand the context of the information they receive. And this context is found offline, in the real world.

Chapter 19
The Third Dimension of Reality

One shouldn't be surprised if a child playing in a park or in the street has a different mindset from a child limited to their room. I am worried about what amount of time a child spends in front of a screen. I feel they are not living a full life, they are living a 2D life.
Baroness Susan Greenfield, English scientist, writer, broadcaster, and member of the House of Lords

In order to cause a shadow to disappear, you must shine light on it.
Shakti Gawain, personal development writer

Is the digital world real? This is clearly a trick question. It is real, because it is there. The proof is that we can all see it, and do so for many hours a day. When we look at someone's page on social media, a battle in a video game, a car for sale on Kijiji, we are not imagining things. What we see is really there on the screen we are looking at. But does the image we see truly reflect reality? We now hear about "augmented reality," which makes it possible to superimpose virtual images on real ones in real time. Furthermore, "virtual reality" can boast of resembling reality ever more closely. **The digital world's obsession with seeming as real as possible is paradoxical. As if its ultimate goal were to reinvent theatre.**

But is the online world, or even virtual reality, truly representative of the real world?

In his work *The Republic*,[136] the Greek philosopher Plato recounts the famous allegory of the cave, which can serve as the perfect metaphor to illustrate the relationship between the

---

[136] Plato. (1888). *The Republic of Plato* (B. Jowett, Trans.) London, United Kingdom: Oxford University Press Warehouse.

real world and the digital one. Thousands of years ago, Plato described the following scene.

Imagine men in a cave with their legs and necks chained from childhood. The chains force them to continually look at a wall in the depths of the cave. Far behind them, near the mouth of the cave, a large fire is lit, emitting light. Between them and the fire, people go back and forth, carrying various objects in front of them. Recall that the prisoners are shackled in such a way that they cannot turn their heads. Thus, they see only the shadows of the people and objects between them and the fire, projected on the wall of the cave. The prisoners cannot see each other either, but they talk together and name the shadows they see—shadows that they believe to be the only "real" things.

Plato reflects on what would happen to one of these prisoners if he were released from his chains and cured of his ignorance by being led into the light. Dazzled by it, he would be unable to perceive the reality of the things that he had only seen as shadows previously. He would struggle to name them, the shadows seeming truer than the objects he would now see.

Plato continues his reflection, "And suppose [...] that he is reluctantly dragged up a steep and rugged ascent, and held fast until he is forced into the presence of the sun himself, is he not likely to be pained and irritated? When he approaches the light his eyes will be dazzled, and he will not be able to see anything at all of what are now called realities." Plato goes on to explain what the consequences would be for the freed prisoner: "He will require to grow accustomed to the sight of the upper world. And first he will see the shadows best, next the reflections of men and other objects in the water, and then the objects themselves; then he will gaze upon the light of the moon and the stars and the spangled heaven; and he will see the sky and the stars by night better than the sun or the light of the sun by day [...]. Last of he will be able to see the sun [...]. He will then proceed to argue that this is [what] gives the seasons and the years, and is the guardian of all that is in the visible world, and in a certain way the cause of all things which he and his fellows have been accustomed to behold." Then, Plato says, the freed prisoner will remember his captive companions and will pity them.

Finally, Plato explains what would occur if this man went back into the depths of the cave and took his place once more: "[...] would he not be certain to have his eyes full of darkness? [...] And if there were a contest, and he had to compete in measuring the shadows with the prisoners who had never moved out of the den, while his sight was still weak, and before his eyes had become steady [...m]en would say of him that up he went and down he came without his eyes; and that it was better not even to think of ascending [...]."

If Plato was among us now, he would be amazed at the relevance of his text. This philosophical text,[137] written 2500 years ago, seems to have been intended as a parody illustrating the current dichotomy of the digital world and the real world. In the allegory of the cave, the conversations between the prisoners strangely resemble those on social media: "[...] they were in the habit of conferring honours among themselves on those who were quickest to observe the passing shadows and to remark which of them went before, and which followed after, and which were together; and who were therefore best able to draw conclusions as to the future [...]."

We must admit that the digital is not simply a reflection of reality. Is the reflection real? Yes, but it is a diluted reality; a shadow of what is far more real. Behind a

---

[137] The metaphysics of Plato's text establishes a dichotomy between sensible reality and the world of Ideas or Forms, a perspective that we will not address in this book.

Facebook, Twitter, or Instagram profile, where a few emojis attempt to summarize a rich depth of emotion, there is a real person, authentic, full of nuances, desires, worries, needs, shadows, and light, which cannot always be reflected on a social media page. There is much more than a smile behind the smiley that a teenager sends over Snapchat or Instagram. There might be a completely opposite emotion: sadness, the need to please, low self-esteem, loneliness, etc. Behind an obscene image on the Internet, there is a real person; there might also be a stolen childhood, a sad story, and maybe even an entire industry that is getting rich off of the image, which often does not truly reflect reality, because it was touched up. Pornography desensitizes our children, distancing them from reality and blinding them to the beauty of sexuality. Sexuality is a powerful language. But if we abuse this language, and do not use it to say things that are contextually appropriate, it loses its meaning entirely. Simone Weil said that "Love needs reality. What is more terrible than the discovery that through a bodily appearance we have been loving an imaginary being. It is much more terrible than· death, for death does not prevent the beloved from having lived. That is the punishment for having fed love on imagination." As Leonardi da Vinci rightly observed, "The ambitious, who are not content with the gifts of life and the beauty of the world, are given the penance of ruining their own lives and never possessing the utility and beauty of the world."

Our children must grow up in the real world, not closed up in the cave with the shadows. They must begin their day by drawing the curtain and looking up at the sky in order to decide how to dress, according to whether the day will be cool, hot, or rainy. Why do they look for this information on their smartphone? The first and last thoughts of their day should not be dedicated to their phone. What a pity that they waste the best years of their life this way, with their eyes glued to a screen!

As the Baroness Susan Greenfield, a British neuroscientist, says, our challenge as parents and teachers, and as society as a whole, is to design an environment in such a way that it is more attractive for a child to be part of the real world, in three dimensions, than to just sit in front of a screen and look at a two-dimensional image. As we said at the beginning of this book, an eighteen-month-old child prefers to see events directly rather than through a screen. This is the proof that reality is powerful enough in itself, because we are born with a sense of wonder that pushes us towards it. Human beings are made to learn from reality. However, a bombardment with information and the fast-paced rhythm of media multitasking can have an impact on this faculty. Children can lose their sense of wonder, their interest in reality. They become captivated by the gratification that digital play offers them. Hence, *the solution should not be to transform reality into something just as fast-paced as what appears on a screen*. An American study[138] that analyzed the content of 59 purportedly educational DVDs, intended for children under the age of 3, counted 7.5 abrupt scene changes per minute. *Attempting to compete with a screen for a young child's attention would mean that our homes and classrooms would have to be transformed into continuous entertainment, rather than places that are suitable for learning.*

The solution lies in experiencing the world directly, not through a screen. Children make sense of reality through everyday things. *Playing with the bubbles in a bath; listening to the crickets sing; counting the stars; stroking*

---

[138] Goodrich, S.A., Pempek, T.A., & Calvert, S.L. (2009). Formal production features of infant and toddler DVDs. *Archives of Pediatrics and Adolescent Medicine, 163*(12), 1.151–1.156.

the skin of a peach; losing themselves in the gaze of a parent; knowing how to read sadness in the face of a friend and in doing so, feel compassion; admiring the reflection of light in raindrops; feeling prickly grass underfoot... No technology can transmit the knowledge that these experiences impart. Reality alone can stir up wonder in our children. Parents and teachers must themselves wonder at the world around them. As Rachel Carson said, "If a child is to keep alive his inborn sense of wonder [...] he needs the companionship of at least one adult who can share it, rediscovering with him the joy, excitement and mystery of the world we live in." In other words, the real world will remain incomprehensible for children or teenagers if they are disconnected from personal sensory experience or interpersonal relationships. Interpersonal relationships are what give meaning to these experiences. When children discover a snail, they immediately seek their parent's gaze in order to understand the importance of their discovery. Without these interpersonal relationships, children become less interested in reality and look for something more "interesting" inside the cave. Contact with the real world should lead children to look for the rainbow when the sun and rain are seen together, or to conclude that it is the sun that causes the seasons and years.

Looking at shadows in a cave is certainly not in itself harmful. It can even be an exotic and interesting activity, if we see it as an excursion for the sake of diversion. However, it is no longer a simple excursion when our youth spent a cumulative total of 4 years and 3 months of their waking hours between the ages of 8 and 18 in the digital world. The problem becomes apparent when children think that eggs come from the refrigerator, when some of them have never seen real cows or rabbits, do not know their smell, the sensation of touching them, the noises they make, or their size, and think that all rabbits look like Bugs Bunny. As psychologist and author Wayne Dyer said, "The highest form of ignorance is when you reject something you don't know anything about." Plato said at the beginning of his allegory of the cave that the prisoners were chained up from their childhood. They did not remember having seen reality, and thus their shadows seemed to them to be what was most real. This is why they did not want to leave the cave. If in the past we had to resort to trickery to get our children to come home at a reasonable hour, now we can barely get them to leave their digitalized bedroom.

Because of the time spent in front of a screen, some children can display a reality deficit. Perhaps this seems a bit exaggerated to us. In fact, for a digital immigrant, the risk of suffering a reality deficit is infinitesimal, because we have experienced the bulk of what we know of the world directly, by means of reality. But they have not. A study[139] published in 2009 reported that, since 1997, people had been spending more time in front of screens than they had interacting with other human beings. We can imagine how the situation has evolved since then.

As we saw earlier, it has been proven that babies and young children learn less from two-dimensional images and more from real-life situations, face-to-face. The *video deficit effect* is attested to by many pediatric studies.[140] What is more, an American study[141] that compared the reaction of babies to the

---

[139] Sigman, A. (2009). Well connected? The biological implications of "social networking". *The Biologist, 56*(1), 14–20.

[140] Among others: Anderson, D.R., & Pempek, T.A. (2005). Television and very young children. *American Behavioral Scientist, 48*, 505–522.

[141] Diener, M.L., Pierroutsakos, S. L., Troseth, G.L., & Roberts, A. (2008). Video versus reality: Infant's attention and affective responses to video and live presentations. *Media Psychology, 11*(3), 418–441.

same event on television and in person concluded that babies hold their gaze longer and show more interest in a real situation than one displayed on a screen. In addition, when they were given a choice between real events or virtual ones, they preferred the real ones.

Children thirst for reality. But if children thirst so much for reality, why do they then ask for screens? It is because screens fascinate them. *Their speed, the flashing lights, and the noise cause children to become passive, captivated, to lose their natural interest in learning, and to end up depending on external stimulation.*

We often hear of the importance of a "digital diet," which consists in moderating technology use at ages when they are perhaps unnecessary. However, we often forget to speak of the importance of giving children beautiful and real alternatives. We are presented with a false dichotomy (prohibition or moderation) rather than envisioning a solution that relies on *excellence* or *beauty*. Our children need to leave their cave and explore reality. What use is it to impose a schedule for watching the shadows if our youth, like the prisoners in the cave, are not freed from their chains and do not go to live a full life outside? The Canadian author Robin Sharma said, "We can easily forgive a child who is afraid of the dark; the real tragedy of life is when men are afraid of the light."[142] And this is the real tragedy to which technological trances have led us. Leading an entire generation of children, with pseudo-educational arguments, to shut themselves up in their virtual caves, far from the light, far from reality, far from beauty, is not seeking the perfection of which our true nature is capable. And consequently, this in no way respects the end and purpose of education.

---

[142] Sharma, R. (1997). *The monk who sold his Ferrari*. HarperCollins Publishing.

Conclusion

[They] were so preoccupied with whether or not they could,
they didn't stop to think if they should.*
Ian Malcolm, *Jurassic Park*

On one hand, the principal pediatric associations plead in favour of limiting technology use in early childhood. According to them, no data support the introduction of technologies at a young age. On the other hand, many parents remain convinced of the importance of introducing technology during early childhood due to the rhetoric of technomyths. Consequently, parents often place pressure on schools and teachers to use technologies in an educational context.

However, ***teachers and schools should make decisions in light of the scientific literature and pediatric recommendations, and apply the universal principles of prudence and caution.*** Scientific information and pediatric recommendations should be properly distributed and technomyths, which can interfere in the decision-making of schools and parents on questions of technology, must not be disseminated. Although the word "innovation" has been in everyone's mouths in the education world for several decades, perhaps because it symbolizes modernity and progress, let us recall that ***novelty is a commercial concept, not a pedagogical one.*** The true nature of a child has its own rhythm; it is not necessary to bombard it with excessive sensory stimulation. Children need, above all, sensory experiences and a secure attachment founded on positive human interactions with a sensitive educator.

It is up to the educator—primarily the parent—to find a balance between what children ask for and what their true nature demands. *Children like candy, but it nevertheless has no nutritional value. The fact that children like digital devices does not necessarily mean they have educational value.* Parents are the primary educators of their children; it is they who know them best, and it is therefore they who are in the best place to know when their children are mature enough to use digital media responsibly. It is parents who best know when their children have demonstrated enough self-control and have developed a sense of relevancy that will allow them to carry out a meaningful search for information. Every child is different and there is no standardized formula that can work for them all. This is why a mass introduction of technology is a mistake. Neither the government, nor the school, nor a neighbour, nor a telecommunications company, nor statistics, nor even the child, can intervene in these decisions that are made, in the end, for the child's well-being.

How have we reached the point where parents consider themselves so unqualified to educate their own children that they entrust fundamental decisions, such as those related to technology use, to third parties who do not even know them? We must recover the sense of competence and self-esteem that have been lost thanks to neuromyths, technomyths, and statistics in so-called educational books that claim to solve everything with ready-made methods and formulas. What other people do or what statistics tell us about it, should not determine, nor even influence, our family decisions.

Nevertheless, in order to make decisions, parents must have access to trustworthy and complete information. And even though we are living in the information age, we have never suffered so much from misinformation.

Why do we not hear about the results of these studies?

In 2006, the American Medical Association's journal, *Archives of Pediatric and Adolescent Medicine,* published an article by Dimitri Christakis, the chief expert on the effects of screens, entitled, "Media as a Public Health Issue." In it, he asked, "Why is it that something that is widely recognized as being so influential and potentially dangerous has resulted in so little effective action? To be sure, there has been some lack of political will to take on the enormously powerful and influential entertainment industry. [...M]edia need to be recognized as a major public health issue."[143]

Manfred Spitzer, a psychiatrist specializing in the effect of technology and the author of the German bestseller *Digitale Demenz*[144] ("Digital Dementia") is of the same mind. He says, "In view of all the negative repercussions of digital media on the mind and body of young people, repercussions that have been demonstrated many times by science, we might ask ourselves why no one is protesting anything or why they have not at least become indignant or irritated. So, why does nothing ever happen? [...] It is true that much is said on the subject, but given that children have no voice at election time, ultimately no one does anything for them. Politicians think about what is good for the banks or the economy, for the middle class or taxpayers, but deep down they are not concerned with what children really need."

---

[143] Christakis, D.A., & Zimmerman, F.J. (2006). Media as a public health issue. *Archives of Pediatric and Adolescent Medicine, 160*, 445–446.

[144] Spitzer, M. (2012). *Digitale Demenz.* Droemer.

The academic experts in neuropediatrics who study the effects of screens in the field are well aware of their potentially harmful effects on children and adolescents. Yet is it not absurd that on one hand, world-class experts alarm us with talk of the consequences and inherent risks in technology use, while, on the other hand, when it comes time to act, we limit ourselves as a society to speaking about "responsible use" and proposing age limits that are curiously similar to the ages of introduction we already see in the statistics? Why are we not bold enough to speak of the importance of reducing screen time and delaying the age of introduction for digital media? How are we going to improve if we continue doing the same thing? As the saying goes, the definition of insanity is doing the same thing over and over again and expecting a different result.

During his presentation to the Quality of Childhood Group in the European Parliament in 2010,[145] Dr. Aric Sigman, a psychologist and neurophysiologist known for his research on the impact of screens, listed the reasons why this information is not disseminated: "Politicians have, for several reasons, a vital interest in people watching screen media. And both doctors and politicians want to be liked by the public. *Telling parents that screen media might damage the health of their children places them in the position of being the bearer of bad news.* [...] Most importantly, it is unnecessary and counterproductive to form a partnership with media industries as a way of reducing children's use of their services. There is a powerful and obvious conflict of interest." Sigman added that the majority of research on the effects of screens is carried out by experts in media studies, who do not

---

[145] Sigman, A. (2010). The impact of screen media on children: A Eurovision   for   Parliament. http://www.allianceforchildhood.eu/files/book2012/QoC%20Book%20 2012%20Chapter-4.pdf

necessarily consider the educational or health impact of screens on children. "Research funds and conferences are often supported by the enormous corporate spending of large technology industries," he says, which places them all squarely in a conflict of interest.

To all these reasons, we could add the very powerful background music of the technological trances, in which no one wants to get caught playing the wrong note, and which neutralizes our efforts to reflect critically and calmly. To this can further be added educational arguments based on neuromyths and technomyths, which are fed by the desire to be "good parents," fooling us into thinking, "the more, the better" when it comes to the use of digital media.

In the presentation quoted above, Sigman gave a summary of hundreds of studies attesting to the negative effects of screens on children, and concluded his presentation by saying, "there is nothing to be lost by children watching less screen media but potentially a great deal to be lost by allowing children to continue to watch as much as they do. By ignoring the growing body of evidence linking screen time with child health we may ultimately be responsible for the greatest health scandal of our time."

Thus, a large part of the solution is to decrease screen time. Sigman has been accused by some of being an alarmist. Time will tell; indeed, it has already had much to say. His warning now almost sounds prophetic. But precisely because we do not know with certainty what all the consequences of this unprecedented situation will be, precaution and responsibility are no doubt in order. Further, *as parents, we should not be motivated by the fear of an eventual catastrophe, but by a desire for our children's excellence*. Acting out of fear leads us to do the bare minimum to avoid getting in trouble instead of proactively seeking out the best for our children. And this is the exact opposite of what education should be.

Our children need to grow up in contact with reality. The beauty of reality. The philosopher Thomas Aquinas said that beauty is in everything. However, in some things there is more, in others less. We must raise our children to have sensitivity and a sense of wonder, which will allow them to recognize the beauty of the real world, so that they will eventually be able to identify and appreciate those of the virtual world. *Our children must experience reality through reality itself, not its shadows.* They must grow in virtue, acquiring these qualities in the real world. Only then will they be able to explore the cave and observe the shadows. Because then they will know that the shadows are only shadows, that in order to not remain captive in them, they need the light—the light of beauty, of reality.

The best preparation for the virtual world is the real world

The advantages of technology for adults are undeniable. Technology can be beneficial in the health sector, for research, for greater work efficiency, in daily life, etc. *It is also undeniable that our children and students will end up using technology when they need it and that they will eventually be mature enough to use it responsibly and meaningfully. But faced with a constantly evolving environment, what young users often lack is an internal locus of control, self-mastery, as well as criteria of relevancy that will allow them to understand the value and originality of the information they find.*

Digital media can only be used responsibly once the user is prepared to do so. If we had to summarize what this preparation involves, in light of everything that has been said, we would recommend:

1) Restricting media multitasking to a minimum, as it can transform our children into desperate "suckers for irrelevancy";

2) Reducing external stimuli that demand constant attention—they extinguish sensitivity and numb the natural sense of wonder;

3) Helping children to develop their strength of will;

4) Placing more importance on altruistic and internal motivations than external ones;

5) Helping them to develop an internal locus of control;

6) Giving meaning to what they learn by providing them with the broader context;

7) Giving them opportunities to establish interpersonal relationships that will allow them to strengthen their secure attachment and sense of self;

8) Offering them genuine alternatives to the virtual world in regard to beauty and aesthetic experiences.

It is not hard to see that none of this can be accomplished online. It is mainly achieved offline. In fact, electronic devices, their applications, and social media only serve to interfere with consolidating the qualities necessary for digital media use. This is why *the best preparation for the online world is the offline world.*

When a teenager or an adult has acquired the necessary maturity for using technology responsibly, digital media can be an amazing tool. We should nonetheless ask ourselves: How many children or teenagers possess this maturity? The more present the above-mentioned traits are, the better prepared they will be to use technology without it affecting their capacity for attention and extinguishing their sense of wonder. The less prepared they are, the more harmful side effects there will be, because the device and its applications will consume their attention and transform them into passive beings, and they will be more prone to developing dependencies or abusive consumption habits.

Recovering context

Nowadays, discussing the importance of thinking critically in education is seen very positively. But how can we claim to think critically in the absence of criteria, of a certain degree of certitude? The mind needs reference points, knowledge, and certainties. This cannot be confused with simple information. Certainties are what allow us to make sense of information. *A good use of technology requires contextual knowledge; yet this is absent from an environment as decontextualized as the Internet.* Snatches of information, devoid of context, without a narrative thread, can attract our attention and fascinate us, but they do not give meaning to learning. This is no doubt why we have never before had so many problems with fake news. Fake news is not a technological problem, but arises from a lack of the contextual knowledge that allows someone to judge what is true or false. The solution is not censorship or restrictions on the freedom of speech, but a better education.

The reality is that critical thinking has little to do with the importance attached to technical digital competencies. As explained earlier, a study on the impact of technology on learning in OECD countries[146] concluded that using a computer beyond the daily average of these countries leads to poorer results and that the skills essential for online navigation

---

[146] Organisation for Economic Co-operation and Development. (2015). *Students, computers and learning: Making the connection.* Paris: OECD.

156

can be acquired with the help of analogue tools. In the same vein, UNESCO[147] has put forward a far more current and relevant concept: that of media and information literacy.

In the absence of a context that provides meaning, attention is scattered and our children become "suckers for irrelevancy." We distract ourselves in many directions and none at the same time, and this is why we are no longer able to find ourselves and end up no longer knowing who we are.

What is able to give meaning to learning? Clearly not the Internet, because it does not provide the context that makes it possible to convert information into knowledge. *It is a solid humanistic education that will enable young learners to make sense of the abundance of information available in the digital world.* Once this education has been acquired, they will be able to consider information an ally; this preparation will permit them to contextualize and understand it.

To whom then, in education, does this role fall; to interpret, contextualize, and give meaning to information in order to impart knowledge, stir up wonder, and elicit sustained attention? It falls to the teacher, of course. A 2007 study conducted by McKinsey[148] compared twenty-five education systems recognized for their success and concluded, "The quality of an educational system will never exceed the quality of its teachers." Policymakers must therefore position themselves to improve the preparation and recognition of teachers, and increase the attention they receive. With the necessary time, tools, and preparation, teachers are the ones

---

[147] United Nations Educational, Scientific and Cultural Organization. (2011). *Alfabetización mediática e informacional: Curriculum para profesores.* Paris, France. Retrieved from www.unesco.org/webworld

[148] Barber, M., & Mourshed, M. (2007). How the world's best-performing school systems came out on top. *McKinsey & Company.* https://www.mckinsey.com/industries/social-sector/our-insights/how-the-worlds-best-performing-school-systems-come-out-on-top

who can give meaning to learning. It is knowledge of the material they teach, as well as genuine interest in their students, that will allow them to impart what they know with passion, emotion, intuition, and sensitivity—qualities that digital technologies will never have, no matter how much Silicon Valley is willing to spend on them. ***Education is a human, not a technological, issue.***

In search of Rule Number One

"Rule Forty-two. All persons more than a mile high to leave the court."

Everybody looked at Alice.

"I'm not a mile high," said Alice.

"You are," said the King.

"Nearly two miles high," added the Queen.

"Well, I shan't go, at any rate," said Alice: "besides, that's not a regular rule: you invented it just now."

"It's the oldest rule in the book," said the King.

"Then it ought to be Number One," said Alice.

The King turned pale, and shut his note-book hastily.

Lewis Carroll, *Alice in Wonderland*

Some things will never change, no matter how much we persist in trying to change them. It is these that are the true "Rule Number Ones" of our world, because they are as old as time. The laws of human nature, much like the fundamental principles that govern the operations of the universe, do not change: We are humans and so also are "digital natives." Their mental capacity is no greater than ours. They are not omniscient and never will be—with or without a smartphone in their pocket. They do not have superpowers and never will. Attention cannot be divided; they cannot therefore carry out multiple tasks at once that require reflection. Freedom does not consist in producing an infinite array of possibilities to which we will never be able to commit. Children need interpersonal relationships as much for developing a sense of personal identity as for their learning. They need to be in contact with beauty and the world, by means of sensitivity. They need friendship, empathy, compassion, and human attention. They need context for meaningful learning. They need to make sense of their actions; the search for sense and meaning is furthermore what leads them to act from an internal motivation. Ultimately, they need reality—and lots of it.

The Horse Whisperer, a bestseller by Nicholas Evans that inspired a movie of the same name, explains that in order to be able to control a horse, one must understand its nature and demand no more from it than it is able to do. ***In education, wisdom, or simply common sense—which is itself a form of wisdom—consists in not imposing rules that run counter to nature and in respecting the rules prescribed by our nature.*** "God always forgives, man sometimes forgives, nature never forgives," as the saying goes. When we abuse what our true nature demands, we end up paying dearly for it. The American author Robert G. Ingersoll said that "There are in nature neither rewards nor punishments—there are consequences." We often have difficulty realizing and accepting this; if we could, we would long ago have brought a lawsuit against our own nature, in order to make it bend to our least desires. We already attempt to live beyond reality; to pass off novelties as having always been part of our nature. Something which would resemble what the king in

Wonderland attempted to do with his Rule Forty-two, by which he drove Alice out of a land created for her.

We often speak of innovation. It is good to have the boldness to question and shake up paradigms that are considered untouchable. However, in order to calmly study the innovation question, without prejudices or interference, we must turn off the background music of the technological trances. Innovation does not consist in always seeking out the "shiny new thing." *Being innovative is being original. Being original is "returning to the origins," as the architect Antoni Gaudí said. And we should not be surprised if returning to the origin involves swimming against the current; this is always necessary when you swim towards a river's source.* This is why innovation cannot merely define itself according to the dictates of fashion.

This return to the origins will lead us to seek what goes beyond passing fads: what has meaning. In order to find meaning, it is enough to be open and expectant in the face of reality. This openness, this expectancy towards reality, is the hallmark of the wise. Bernard of Clairvaux, the famous French abbot, said that "Wise is he who sees things as they are."

It was taken for granted that technology would revolutionize education. However, technology has not kept its promise. Nor will it ever do so. Why? *Education is not genuine simply by virtue of being innovative; it is rather innovative by virtue of being genuine.* And education is genuine to the extent that it contemplates and aspires to the perfection *that our nature is able to attain.* This perfection is what gives meaning to what our children learn, to our incredible and indispensable mission as parents and teachers: inspiring our children to wonder at the beauty and splendour of reality.

Author's biography

Catherine L'Ecuyer is Canadian, now living in Barcelona with her four children. She holds a law degree, has an MBA, an Official European Master of Research and a Doctorate in Education and Psychology.

The Swiss journal Frontiers in Human Neuroscience published her article "The Wonder Approach to Learning," which converted her thesis into a new hypothesis/theory of learning. She received the 2015 Pajarita Award from the Spanish Association of Toy Manufacturers for "promoting a culture of play in the media," she was invited to speak to the Education Commission of the Congress of Deputies of Spain and at the Second Summit of Education organized by the European Commission. She has served as a consultant to the Spanish government regarding the use of digital technology by minors, to the government of the state of Puebla in Mexico concerning preschool reform and has participated in a report for the Cerlac (Unesco) on the use of digital media in childhood. In 2020, she has been part of a coalition of 100 international experts calling on educators and policymakers to limit screen time for students led by the Campaign for a commercial-free childhood.

Author of many publications, she is also the bestseller author of The Wonder Approach, published in eight languages and available in more than 40 countries. She currently collaborates with the Mind-Brain Group of the University of Navarra and is a columnist for El País, one of the most-read newspapers in Spanish.

To contact the author:

agenda@catherinelecuyer.com
www.catherinelecuyer-eng.com

Manufactured by Amazon.ca
Bolton, ON